OCR Ethics Revision (

H573/2 (complete two-yea ...se)

By Peter Baron

Published by Active Education

www.peped.org

First published in 2018

ISBN: 9781976991769

Cartoons used with permission © Becky Dyer

All images © their respective owners

Links, reviews, news and revision materials available on www.peped.org

www.peped.org website allows students and teachers to explore Philosophy of Religion and Ethics through handouts, film clips, presentations, case studies, extracts, games and academic articles.

Pitched just right, and so much more than a text book, here is a place to engage with critical reflection whatever your level. Marked student essays are also posted.

Contents

The Examination

The OCR Ethics Course seeks to connect **NORMATIVE THEORIES** to **APPLIED** topics, two in year 1 - euthanasia and business ethics, and one in Year 2 (sexual ethics) Norms are produced by the key moral theories of Utilitarianism, Situation Ethics, Kantian ethics and Natural Law. We are required to apply Natural Law and Situation Ethics to issues surrounding euthanasia, and Kant and Utilitarianism to business ethics. All theories must be used in the consideration of **SEXUAL ETHICS**. Then we ask (in Year 2) what is the foundation of ethics (**META-ETHICS**) and how does **CONSCIENCE** guide us, and where does it come from?

- **CASE STUDIES** are an excellent way of thinking through issues surrounding applied ethics - such as Diane Pretty in 2002 (euthanasia) or Enron in 2003 (business ethics). You will find these on the website www.peped.org

- **MAPPING THE THEORIES** gives a sequence of thought which goes from a starting point (such as **SYNDERESIS** for Natural Law) to a finishing point (**EUDAIMONIA** for Natural Law) and then links the concepts together to form an analysis.

- **TEXTBOOKS** may have their place, but you are examined on the syllabus alone, so study it carefully. There are many ways of doing and thinking about ethics. Wilcockson and Wilkinson (2016) frequently take a Roman Catholic perspective (eg quotes from encyclicals and the Catholic Catechism). But you could just as well quote from the Church of England, the United Reformed Church or the Baptist or Orthodox churches to gain a Christian perspective. Or line up a humanist or atheist perspective against it. Textbooks also include extra material which is not strictly necessary to be an A grade candidate.

- Finally we need to concentrate on the skills of **ANALYSIS** and **EVALUATION**. The specification **OCR H573** is actually quite brief and relatively few authors are named. It is up to the student to select which additional authors to study in order to evaluate properly, and which academic critics to take in considering how to analyse and evaluate each topic. For example, the specification does not mention the theories of **CONSCIENCE** (section 5) of **BUTLER** and Newman, but I have retained them to aid analysis and evaluation of authors that are named (**AQUINAS** and **FREUD**). Similarly, the meta-ethical theory of **PRESCRIPTIVISM** isn't mentioned in the specification, but I feel that in order to evaluate **EMOTIVISM** properly (which is named) we need to consider **PRESCRIPTIVISM** as amore complete theory of how moral language functions.

Introduction to Ethics

Key Terms

- **NORMATIVE ETHICS** - how norms (values of good and bad) are derived and then applied to the real world.

- **META-ETHICS** - the meaning and function of ethical language.

- **OBJECTIVE TRUTH** - the view that truth is testable by observation and experience.

- **RELATIVISM** - the view that all values (norms) are simply expressions of culture and there are no universal, unchanging values of 'good'.

- **SUBJECTIVE TRUTH** - the view that truth is something that depends on an individual perception or belief system and cannot be shared objectively.

- **SITUATION ETHICS** - what is good or bad needs to be assessed according to what maximises love in any situation.

- **TELEOLOGICAL ETHICS** - focuses on the end or telos of an action, for example, Situation Ethics focuses on love.

- **DEONTOLOGICAL** - ethics that focuses on the duty (deon) or rule.

Structure of Thought

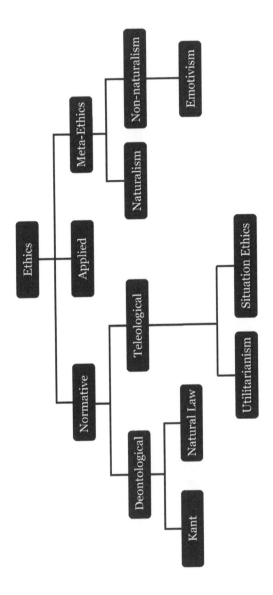

Normative Ethics

Asks the question "how should I act, morally speaking?" or "what ought I to do?"

A **NORM** is a "value" i.e. something I think of as good. The normative theories we study at AS or Year 1 (OCR) are: Natural Law, Kantian ethics, Utilitarianism and Situation Ethics. Each theory derives the idea of goodness a different way: **NATURAL LAW** with reference to the true rational purpose of human beings; **UTILITARIANISM**, with reference to the one assumed norm of happiness and its maximisation; **KANTIAN ETHICS,** by an a priori method of taking an imaginative step backwards and universalising our action; and **SITUATION ETHICS** by maximising the one norm of love in a given situation.

Meta-ethics

META-ETHICS studies the foundations of ethics and meaning of ethical terms (what does it mean to say something is good?). It particularly focuses on ethical language. Key meta-ethical questions include:

- "Is morality absolute – applying everywhere and for all time, or is it relative, specific to a time and place – a culture, situation or viewpoint?"

- "Is there such a thing as a moral fact?"

- "What do different ethical theorists mean by 'good'?"

- "Is goodness a natural feature of the world to be accessed and measured (a bit like science)?"

Applied Ethics

Applies ethical theories to real world situations. The applied issues at AS or Year 1 (OCR) are:

- **Euthanasia applied to Natural Law and Situation Ethics**

- **Business Ethics applied to Utilitarianism and Kantian ethics.**

- **Sexual ethics is studied in Year 2 and all Year 1 normative theories are required.**

A key question in applied ethics is: how do I apply the norm derived by any one ethical theory to the issues surrounding euthanasia and business ethics? The syllabus helps us identify these issues: sanctity of human life, quality of life and autonomy for euthanasia, and globalisation, whistle-blowing, and the interests of stakeholders for business ethics. We could also add our own, such as **SLIPPERY SLOPE** arguments in euthanasia and environmental responsibility for business.

Moreover, we can ask the question generally: is there any difference between an **ACT** (doing something deliberately) and an **OMISSION** (failing to do something)? For example, in cases of euthanasia is failing to offer life support the same ethically as deliberately administering a drug that will kill?

Deontological

Acts are right or wrong in themselves (intrinsically) – it is not about consequences. Often stresses the rules or duty (Kantian ethics is pure deontology and Natural Law has both teleological and deontological aspects). **DEON** is Greek for duty.

Teleological

Teleological theories (**TELOS** = end in Greek) focuses on the purpose and consequences of actions. An action is good only if it brings about beneficial consequences and so fulfils the good purpose (it is instrumentally good, not intrinsically because actions are **MEANS** to some other **END** like happiness or pleasure), for example, Utilitarianism (good purpose is maximising happiness) and Situation Ethics (good purpose is maximising agape love). Joseph Fletcher declares: "the end justifies the means, nothing else".

Four Questions to Ask of Ethical Theories

- **Derivation**: How does the moral theory derive (produce) the idea of goodness?

- **Application**: How can we apply the "good" to choices we make, such as Natural Law to euthanasia or Kantian ethics to business?

- **Realism**: How realistic is the theory with reference to human psychology and our own experience?

- **Motivation**: Why should I be moral? How does this ethical theory suggest I should be motivated to save a stranger in need? What stops me living my life as an ethical egoist, just putting my self-interest first?

These questions will be answered for all moral theories in the final chapter.

Key Quotes - Norms

"There are no absolute universal moral standards binding on all men at all times". John Ladd

"All men are created equal..they are endowed with certain unalienable rights". US Declaration of Independence

"Values are merely culturally approved habits". Ruth Benedict

"In its nature, the moral judgement is wholly independent of religion". William Temple

"The end justifies the means, nothing else". Joseph Fletcher

"There is no objective truth". J.L.Mackie

"We are in danger of falling into a tyranny of relativism". Pope Benedic

The only good thing is the good will". Immanuel Kant

"There could still be a set of general moral norms applicable to all cultures and even recognised in most, which a culture could disregard at its own expense". Louis Pojman

"The Gentiles have the law written on their hearts, to which their conscience bears witness". Romans 2:14

Natural Law

NATURAL LAW is a normative **DEONTOLOGICAL** theory coming from a **TELEOLOGICAL** worldview, as Aristotle argues that the good is defined by the **RATIONAL ENDS** (telos = end) or **FINAL CAUSES** which people by nature pursue.

"Natural Law is the sharing in the eternal law by intelligent creatures" argues **AQUINAS** and calls these rational ends **OBJECTS OF THE WILL**. Key assumptions are that we have a fixed human nature, there is an eternal law in God himself, and the **SYNDERESIS** principle – that all human beings naturally share a conscience that guides us to "do good and avoid evil". Aquinas calls synderesis "the **FIRST PRINCIPLE** of the natural law" and it is one of two words he uses for conscience.

Key Terms

- **NATURAL LAW** - "right reason in agreement with nature", (Cicero). "The sharing in the eternal law by rational creatures', (Aquinas).

- **SYNDERESIS** - the first principle that we by nature seek to do good and avoid evil – or have an innate knowledge of first principles (the primary precepts). This makes the theory universal in application (it applies to a Christian believer and a non-believer or believer of another religion).

- **PRIMARY PRECEPTS** - principles known innately which define the rational ends or goods of human existence and define the good goals we pursue - these are general and do not change.

- **SECONDARY PRECEPTS** - applications of the primary precepts using human reason, which are not absolute and so may change. For example, the Catholic church may revise its absolute ban on contraception as a violation of the precept of reproduction.

- **APPARENT GOODS** - acts done from reason which do not correspond to the natural law.

- **REAL GOODS** - acts done from human reason which correspond to the natural law.

- **NATURAL RIGHTS** - rights given to human beings because of their very nature as human. These are enshrined in the US Declaration of Independence which starts: 'we hold these rights to be inalienable'.

- **ETERNAL LAW** - the law as conceived by God and existing as an ideal of all law and projected in the design of the Universe.

- **DIVINE LAW** - the law revealed to humankind in the Bible, such as the ten commandments in the book of Exodus or the beatitudes in Matthew.

- **HUMAN LAW** - the laws we establish by human reason as our social laws.

Structure of Thought

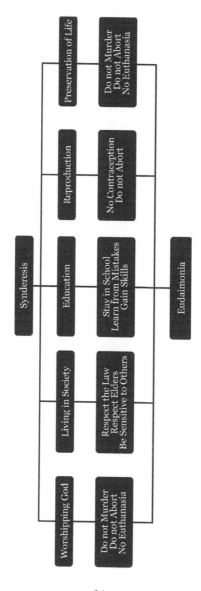

Synderesis: 'each precious child, born with the desire to do good, and avoid evil'

Aquinas' Argument

AQUINAS sought to reconcile Christian thought with Greek thinking (**ARISTOTLE**'s works) discovered in Islamic libraries at the **FALL OF TOLEDO** (1085), when Christian armies reconquered Spain.

He sees goodness in the **DIVINE ESSENCE** (nature of God) which has a purpose – the **ETERNAL LAW** – reflected in our **HUMAN NATURE** and the ends we rationally pursue. A key assumption Aquinas makes is called the **SYNDERESIS** principle that we naturally "do good and avoid evil" –

which is the opposite of the **REFORMATION** assumption that "all have sinned and fall short of God's glory" (Romans 3:23).

We are born with good natures, able to reason and so pursue good ends or objects of the will. The **DIVINE LAW** reflects God's eternal law and is revealed in holy Scripture (eg Ten Commandments of Exodus 20). From these observable God-designed rational ends (goals) we get the **PRIMARY PRECEPTS**.

Primary Precepts

There are five observable "goods" or rational ends we pursue. (Acronym **POWER**).

- **P**reservation of life

- **O**rdered society

- **W**orship of God

- **E**ducation

- **R**eproduction

These reflect the **DIVINE WILL** because God designed us with a rational nature in His image. Notice that **VERITATIS SPLENDOR** (1995 Papal document) has changed the emphasis – Worship of God becomes **APPRECIATION OF BEAUTY** (to fit with our agnostic age), and it adds concern for the environment to reflect the new emphasis on stewardship rather than **DOMINION** (Genesis 1:24 "and let man have dominion over the earth"). Note that the commitment to environmental value is weak in Veritatis Splendor: "to preserve and cultivate the riches of the natural world'. These subtle changes may indicate that Natural Law is not as **ABSOLUTE** as we sometimes think. The fourth type of law is **HUMAN LAW**.

For society to flourish (Greek telos (purpose) of **EUDAIMONIA** sees happiness as personal and social flourishing) we need to bring our human law in line with the **ETERNAL LAW** of God, or put another way, make it appropriate for rational human beings to fulfil their Godly destiny – being with God forever, and being Christlike.

The Four Laws

Natural Law can be mapped in two ways. The first way is **TELEOLOGICAL**   because it focuses on the end or telos of human behaviour - to achieve a flourishing or fulfilled life, **EUDAIMONIA** (see mindmap). Aristotle begins Nichomachean Ethcis by arguing 'the intrinsic good is that at which all things aim' - a broad and general goal.

The second way is by focusing on duties created by the four laws.

• **ETERNAL LAW** - a blueprint in the mind of God of the principles by which God made and controls the universe, which we discover by observation **A POSTERIORI** - through scientific experiments for example, or **A PRIORI** by pure reason as in Mathematics.

- **NATURAL LAW** - the moral law inherent in human beings, discoverable by reason, and expressed in the rational goals which humans by nature pursue.

- **DIVINE LAW** - expressed in the Bible (eg the Ten Commandments or Sermon on the Mount) and then interpreted and applied by human reason.

- **HUMAN LAW** - formulated as codes that create the common good and the precept of an ordered society, and should reflect the eternal law in order to be seen to be good and just. If a ruler ordered that we kill all female babies this would be bad for human flourishing and contrary to the **PRMARY PRECEPT** of preservation of life. and so an unjust and 'bad' law.

These can be represented as a diamond with eternal law at the top. Note that we 'are only required to obey secular rulers to the extent that justice requires' (Aquinas). Evil laws should be resisted and disobeyed.

Secondary Precepts

These are **APPLICATIONS** of the **PRIMARY PRECEPTS** and may change eg as our society changes, science advances our understanding of the Divine Mind, or a situation demands it (eg Thou shalt not kill gets suspended in times of war).

Aquinas suggests **POLYGAMY** (many wives) may sometimes be justified. We don't necessarily have to accept Roman Catholic applications eg Abortion is tantamount to murder, Euthanasia breaks the **SANCTITY OF LIFE**, contraception goes against the primary natural purpose of sex, which is **REPRODUCTION**, and homosexual behaviour is described as **INTRINSICALLY DISORDERED** (the phrase used in **HUMANAE VITAE**, 1968).

There is another assumption here, that there is one human nature – heterosexual- and so there can't be a gay nature. Modern Psychology (eg Carl **JUNG**) suggests we have male and female aspects to our natures and Chinese philosophy has always talked in terms of **YING** and **YANG** – the two aspects of our nature.

Phronesis

Practical wisdom (**PHRONESIS** in Greek) is important because we need to cultivate right judgment to identify the non-absolute **SECONDARY PRECEPTS**. "Practical wisdom turns the application into action, which is the goal of practical reason" (Aquinas). So Natural Law has a situational aspect - we need to assess and 'the more specific the conditions are, the greater the probability of an exception arising', argues Aquinas (ST I -II q. 94 a.4c). **SYNDERESIS** gives us a general orientation towards the good but **PHRONESIS** fills in the details of how to apply any primary precept.

Apparent Goods

We cannot consciously sin because our nature is such that we believe we are "doing good and avoiding evil" – the **SYNDERESIS** principle – even when practising genocide. However, though we rationalise it, this clearly breaks the **ETERNAL LAW** reflected in the **NATURAL LAW** that most rational humans want to **PRESERVE LIFE** (primary precept **P** of **POWER** acronym above). We cannot flourish if we break the Natural Law – in this sense we are being sub-human and irrational (even though we believe otherwise). **AQUINAS** calls these **APPARENT GOODS** – which we mistakenly believe (eg Hitler's genocide) are **REAL GOODS**. We can sin, but not consciously, which is why Evangelical Christians dislike Natural Law theory – arguing it is unrealistic (our very reason is distorted by sin) and unbiblical (it seems to deny Paul's teaching on **ORIGINAL SIN**, inherited from Adam after the **FALL** in Genesis 3).

Two Goods in Conflict

In business ethics the principles of truthfulness and loyalty to the company come into conflict when a whistleblower discovers evidence of wrongdoing, or with euthanasia, when doctors increase the morphine dose to alleviate pain in the knowledge that they will kill the patient. **DOUBLE EFFECT** argues that if the primary effect results from a good intention (alleviate suffering) then the secondary effect isn't evil (causing a death). Notice you can only make the judgement by considering **CONSEQUENCES** and the end of patient welfare. Aquinas argues:

27

"moral actions take their character from what is intended" and so if I act in self defence and unintentionally kill someone I am not doing wrong as long as the action is **PROPORTIONATE.**

Strengths

AUTONOMOUS AND RATIONAL: Natural law is an autonomous, rational theory and it is wrong to say that you have to believe in God to make sense of it. Aquinas speaks of "the pattern of life lived according to reason". You could be a Darwinian atheist and believe in natural law derived by empirical observation, with the primary precept of survival (Aquinas' preservation of life). Richard **DAWKINS** (The Selfish Gene) goes so far as to argue for a natural genetic tendency to be altruistic: a lust to be nice. "The theory of Natural Law suggests..morality is **AUTONOMOUS.** It has its own questions, its own methods of answering them, and its own standards of truth, and religious considerations are not the point". Rachels (2006:56)

AN EXALTED VIEW OF HUMAN BEINGS: We use reason to work out how to live. So we are not slaves to our passions or our genes. Natural Law has a purpose: a flourishing society and a person fulfilled and happy - **EUDAIMONIA**. It is not ultimately about restricting us by rules, but setting us free to fulfil our proper purpose or **TELOS**, inherent in our design: to rationally assent to personal growth. If we can agree on our purpose we can agree on what morality is for. Moreover, we don't have to accept the fact/value division inherent in Moore or Ayer's philosophy.

"The natural world is not to be regarded merely as a realm of facts, devoid of value or purpose. Instead, the world is conceived to be a **RATIONAL ORDER** with value and purpose built into its very nature". Rachels (2006: 50)

FLEXIBLE: Natural Law is not inflexible. The primary precepts may be general and unchanging, but as Aquinas argued, **SECONDARY PRECEPTS** can change depending on circumstances, culture and worldview. Aquinas calls them 'proximate conclusions of reason'. The Doctrine of **DOUBLE EFFECT** is also a way to escape the moral dilemmas which exist when two rules conflict, (See Louis Pojman 2006: 47-51) – so not as **ABSOLUTE** as textbooks suggest.

Weaknesses

A FIXED HUMAN NATURE: Aquinas believes in one fixed, shared human nature with certain natural properties eg heterosexual. But evidence suggests there are gay genes and so there is no one natural human nature, but many. This is actually a form of the **NATURALISTIC FALLACY**, the movement from an "is" to an "ought". "It may be that sex does produce babies, but it does not follow that sex ought or ought not to be engaged in only for that purpose. Facts are one thing, values are another". Rachels (2006:52)

AN OPTIMISTIC VIEW: Aquinas believes that we **INNATELY** (we are born with) have a "tendency to do good and avoid evil", **SYNDERESIS**. This is in contrast with Augustine who believes that, due to the Fall, we are born into sin, the sin of Adam, or perhaps the view of psychologists like Freud, that natural selfishness becomes moralised by upbringing and socialisation.

IMMORAL OUTCOMES: Natural Law has been interpreted to ban contraception, because this interferes with the natural primary precept of reproduction. But a. it's not clear that sex is exclusively for reproduction, in fact, the function of bonding may be primary and b. the consequence of this policy in Africa has had evil effects of the spread of **AIDS** and the birth of **AIDS** infected children who often become orphans living on the streets.

Confusions - Natural Law

1. "Natural" means "as we see in the natural world". This isn't true because many things we see in the natural world we would argue are **IMMORAL** (eg killing the weak which animals do all the time). "Natural" means something closer to "**APPROPRIATE** for our rational human nature", for example, we may naturally feel lust but it is **IRRATIONAL** and wrong to seek to indulge this lust with a complete stranger.

2. "Natural law is dogmatic and inflexible". This is a wrong reading of Aquinas who himself argues that the **SECONDARY PRECEPTS** are liable to change with circumstances and our developed understanding. It is quite possible to be a Natural Law theorist and argue in favour of contraception on the grounds that

it is necessary to save lives and reduce destructive population growth. Roman Catholic interpretations are open to debate.

3. "Natural Law is deontological". This is an overstatement as Natural Law is profoundly **TELEOLOGICAL** in its goal of eudaimonia and follows the Greek teleological worldview. However, it is still law, and is enshrined in principles and rules and codes of law which should reflect the **ETERNAL LAW** of God. The laws have to be **JUST** and subject to right reason.

4. "Natural Law requires God". Aquinas rejects **DIVINE COMMAND THEORY** (the argument that something is good or bad because God commands it). Natural Law therefore does not require God but is knowable by reason alone and observable in nature. Christian Natural Law theory argues that the divine blueprint for the Universe is reflected in its design and discoverable by scientific research, as well as reflection on the proper rational purposes of human beings.

Possible Exam Questions

1. "Natural Law does not present a helpful method for making moral decisions". Discuss

2. "Moral decisions should be based on duty, not purpose". Assess with reference to the theory of Natural Law.

3. "Human beings are born with the tendency to pursue morally good ends". Evaluate in the light of teleological aspects of Natural Law.

4. "Explain and justify the doctrine of double effect with reference to an ethical dilemma of your choice concerning euthanasia".

Key Quotes - Natural Law

"The natural law is the sharing in the eternal law by intelligent creatures". Thomas Aquinas

"For Aquinas, the basis of the moral life is prudence, right practical reason in the pursuit of charity". Herbert McCabe

"The order of the precepts of the natural law is the order of our natural inclinations". Thomas Aquinas

"Our ultimate end is unrelated good, namely God, who alone can fill our will to the brim because of infinite goodness". Thomas Aquinas

"The natural law is unchangeable in its first principles, but in its secondary principles it may be changed through some special causes hindering the following of the primary precepts". Thomas Aquinas

"The natural law involves universality as it is inscribed in the rational nature of a person. It makes itself felt in every person endowed with reason". Veritatis Splendor (1995)

"Every marital act must of necessity retain its intrinsic relationship to the procreation of human life". Humanae Vitae (1968)

"The theory of Natural law suggests morality is autonomous. It has its own questions, its own methods of answering them and its own standards of truth. Religious considerations are not the point". James Rachels

"The world is conceived as a rational order with value and purpose built into its very nature". James Rachels

"Nature inclines to that which is necessary for the perfection of community". Thomas Aquinas

Kantian Ethics

Background

KANT aimed to produce a **COPERNICAN REVOLUTION** in Ethics, by arguing that moral principles can be derived **A PRIORI** (by abstract reasoning) in contrast with the Utilitarian **A POSTERIORI** (experiential) method. Both are children of the **ENLIGHTENMENT** whose method is 'dare to reason'. David **HUME** awoke Kant from his 'dogmatic slumbers' by showing how a freely thinking philosopher can transform the way we look at things, including morality.

Key Terms

• **AUTONOMY** freedom to reason about the moral law

• **CATEGORICAL** unconditional, absolute, with no 'ifs"

• **HYPOTHETICAL** conditional, relative to circumstances, with 'ifs'

• **SUMMUM BONUM** the greatest good, combining virtue and happiness

• **DUTY** the sole moral motive of pursuing a line of action because it is right, whether or not we feel like it

Structure of thought

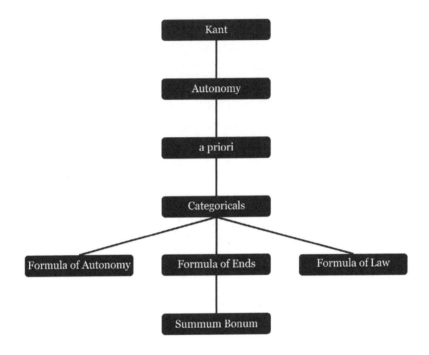

Deontological

A **NORMATIVE** theory (tells you what is right and wrong/what you ought to do), that is **DEONTOLOGICAL** (acts are intrinsically right and wrong in themselves, stressing rules and duties), **ABSOLUTIST** (applies universally in all times, places, situations) and is **A PRIORI** (derived from reason alone, not experience).

Autonomy

The key Kantian assumption is that we are **AUTONOMOUS** moral agents (self-ruled) which have free choice and free reason, rather than **HETERONOMOUS** meaning "ruled by others", where the others could be God, your peer group, or the Church. Kant adopted the **ENLIGHTENMENT** slogan "dare to reason" and was awakened out of his slumbers by reading Jean-Jacques **ROUSSEAU**'s theory of the social contract.

Good Will

Kant argues that the only thing that is morally good without exception is the **GOOD WILL**. A person of good will is someone motivated by **DUTY** alone. They are not motivated by self-interest, happiness or a feeling of sympathy. The good will is an **INTRINSIC** good (it is good in itself and not as a means to something else) and it doesn't matter if it doesn't bring about good consequences. Even if the good will achieved nothing good –

even if it were combined with all manner of other evils — "it would shine forth like a jewel, having full value in itself". He contrasts this with other qualities (such as courage) which **CAN** be good but might also be bad depending on the situation (eg a courageous suicide bomber) which are **EXTRINSIC** goods as they depend on the circumstances.

Duty

Kant argues that we must follow our duty. It is not about what we want to do (our **INCLINATIONS**) or what will lead to the best consequences: only the action which springs from duty is a moral action. Doing your duty (eg helping a beggar) may be pleasurable, but this cannot be the reason why you did your duty (the **MOTIVE**). For it to be moral you have to act because it is your duty, and **FOR NO OTHER REASON**.

Categorical Imperative (C.I.)

How do you know what your duty is? Kant argues that this comes from the **CATEGORICAL IMPERATIVE**. It is categorical because it applies to us universally — simply because we have rational wills. By contrast a **HYPOTHETICAL IMPERATIVE** takes the form "If you want X, then you must do Y" (eg if you want to lose weight, then you must stop eating so much). The difference is the categorical imperative applies to us unconditionally, without any reference to a goal we might have (it is simply the form "You must do Y").

C.I. 1 THE FORMULA OF LAW

"So act that the maxim of your action may be willed as a universal law for all humanity". For any action to be moral, you must be able to **CONSISTENTLY UNIVERSALISE** it. For example, if you decide not to keep a promise, then you must be able to consistently imagine a world where **EVERYONE** doesn't keep their promises – something Kant thought was impossible (because then no-one would believe a promise and so promise-keeping would vanish). He calls this a **CONTRADICTION IN NATURE** because the very nature of the thing – promising – is destroyed and so the action becomes self-contradictory.

C.I. 2 FORMULA OF ENDS

"Never treat people simply as a means to an end but always also as an end in themselves". People are **RATIONAL** and **AUTONOMOUS** (self-legislators) and so are worthy of respect. We cannot ONLY use them as a means for getting something else, but always as rational beings with dignity. We universalise our common humanity – which means we treat others as equals, with rights.

C.I.3 FORMULA OF AUTONOMY

Kant imagines a community of purely rational agents, each of whom is a **LEGISLATOR** (someone who decides laws) and a **SUBJECT** (someone who has to follow those laws) in what he calls a **KINGDOM OF ENDS**. We can only act on moral laws that would be accepted by this fully rational community – we belong to a moral parliament where we are free participators in the law-making process. This introduces an important

SOCIAL aspect to Kantian ethics. "Kantian ethics is the ethics of democracy". James Rachels

Summum Bonum

The **SUMMUM BONUM** or "supreme good" is **VIRTUE** (a person of 'good will' who follows their duty by applying the Categorical Imperative) combined with **HAPPINESS**. We should not act in order to get happiness (because moral action should only involve doing our duty for duty's sake), but the ideal is that we should be happy to the degree that we **DESERVE** to be happy. This is obviously not something that can be found in this life – we see bad people living happy lives and good people living unhappy lives – therefore the Summum Bonum must be able to be achieved in the **AFTERLIFE**.

Three Postulates

Kant argued there are three necessary **POSTULATES** (or propositions which we **ASSUME** rather than **PROVE**) for morality:

1. **FREEDOM** (we must be free to make moral decisions)

2. **IMMORTALITY** (there must be an afterlife in order to achieve the summum bonum).

3. **GOD** (necessary to guarantee the moral law and to judge fairly and reward or punish).

Strengths

It's **REASONABLE** – pretty much what most people consider morality to be about (ie universalising your behaviour). The various formulations of the Categorical Imperative take the **DIGNITY** and **EQUALITY** of human beings very seriously. The innocent are protected by the universal equality given to all human beings.

Weaknesses

It is **INFLEXIBLE** as absolutes have to be applied in all situations irrespective of what we consider to be the wisest choice. Kant also seems to make a clear distinction between our **EMOTIONS** and the ethical choice done from duty alone - but is it really morally doubtful if I act out of emotion like compassion and not just from **DUTY** alone? Also, what happens when two duties **CONFLICT** (eg I need to lie to a crazy knifeman who is enquiring if my friend is in the house - Kant's own example where he insists we tell the truth whatever happens). Surely **CONSEQUENCES** do matter, and arguably there has to be a consequential element to Kant when we imagine universalising an imperative.

Notice that the weaknesses may also be **STRENGTHS** in certain circumstances - such as a difficult choice which may affect human lives whichever way we choose.

Confusions - Kant

1. "Duty means blind obedience". This is what Adolf Eichmann implied in his trial in 1962 - but it's not Kant's view of duty which involves reasoning through the **UNIVERSALISABILITY** of your action and treating all human beings with equal respect.

2. "Duty means ignoring emotion". This is a possible reading of Kant, but not the only one. Another reading is to say that Kant saw **DUTY** as the primary motive and so long as emotions don't conflict with duty then having moral emotions is fine - just don't base your reason on emotion as it is unreliable.

3. 'Kantian ethics is deontological". William Frankena classified Kant as deontological and it is true Kant argues for unconditional

commands (categoricals). But when we universalise we can't help thinking about consequences - there is a consequential dimension to Kant. Whether we have done our duty from the right motive is deontological - but determining the right duty needs a **TELEOLOGICAL** approach.

Possible Exam Questions

1. "Kantian ethics is not helpful in providing practical guidelines for making moral decisions". Discuss

2. Evaluate to what extent duty can be the sole basis for a moral action.

3. "Kantian ethics is too abstract to be useful in practical ethical decision-making'. Discuss

4. "In neglecting the role of emotions in favour of pure reason, Kantian ethics fails to give a realistic account for our human nature". Discuss

Key Quotes - Kant

"It is impossible to conceive of anything in the world good without qualification except the good will". Immanuel Kant

"Two things fill me with wonder, the starry hosts above and the moral law within". Immanuel Kant

"Kant places the stern voice of duty at the heart of the moral life". Robert Arrington

"If our moral sense were based merely on feelings, it would not only vary from person to person – just as some gentlemen prefer blondes and others don't – but could also vary within a person according to his state of health and experiences". Peter Rickman

"There remain the categorical imperatives, which derive their authority from reason itself; and the only thing reason abstracted from actual information about specific conditions can command is consistency." Peter Rickman

"The highest created good is a world where rational beings are happy and worthy of happiness". Immanuel Kant

"To have any goal of action is an act of freedom". Immanuel Kant

"With sufficient ingenuity almost every precept can be consistently universalised". Alasdair MacIntyre

"There is more to the moral point of view than being willing to universalise one's rules". William Frankena

Bentham's Act Utilitarianism

Background

The Utilitarians attempted to bring **SCIENCE** to morality by producing an **EMPIRICAL** (testable) method to establishing right and wrong. The approach is **RADICAL** in two senses - there is a radical **EQUALITY** in its method and a radical **SIMPLICITY** which works especially well when assessing **PUBLIC POLICY** (eg whether to reduce road congestion or have legislation pro **EUTHANASIA**). Bentham wanted a new **PRISONS** policy which was centred on character reform, and **MILL** was briefly imprisoned for campaigning for **CONTRACEPTION**. A central difficulty remains: what happens if torturing you makes everyone else happier? Utilitarians argue for **NET** happiness to be **MAXIMISED** (total **PLEASURE** minus total **PAIN**).

Key Terms

- **PLEASURE** the one intrinsic good, according to Bentham

- **GREATEST HAPPINESS PRINCIPLE** to act to maximise the greatest happiness of the greatest number - the fundamental principle of utilitarian ethics

- **HEDONIC CALCULUS** a way of quantifying pleasure by seven criteria

- **TELEOLOGICAL** a theory which relates goodness to ends or purposes

- **CONSEQUENTIALIST** identifying goodness by the results of an action

- **EMPIRICAL** a scientific word implying morality can be tested and measured

Background

BENTHAM (1748-1832) was a social reformer who believed that the law should serve human needs and welfare. Where **JUSTICE** was **RETRIBUTIVE** he wanted to see it **REFORMING** the person and acting as a **DETERRENCE** – there had to be a real social benefit outweighing the pain to the criminal, and with a better **DISTRIBUTION** of resources, but all in the cause of the **GREATEST HAPPINESS PRINCIPLE (GHP)** – the motive was to reduce suffering and increase happiness for everyone. The theory is **TELEOLOGICAL** because it measures likely consequences of **ACTIONS**, and **HEDONIC** because Bentham believed pleasure (Greek: hedon) was the key motive and could be quantified. So there is an **EMPIRICAL**, objective measure of goodness.

Structure of Thought

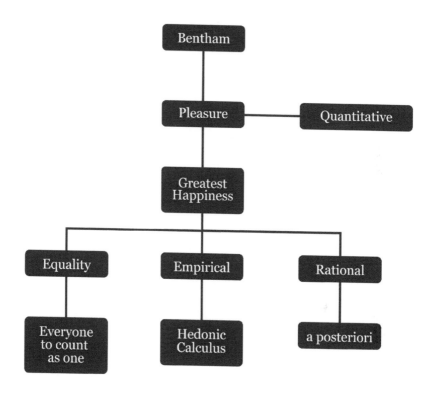

Motivation

There is one **MORAL** good – pleasure, and one evil – pain. "Nature has placed mankind under two **SOVEREIGN** masters, pain and pleasure". Right actions are on balance pleasurable, wrong actions are on balance painful. Bentham's is therefore a theory of **PSYCHOLOGICAL HEDONISM** (Hedonism - pleasure-seeking).

Hedonic Calculus

The **HEDONIC CALCULUS** is a way of measuring pleasure and pain, so the consequences of an act can be assessed as a score in units of happiness called **HEDONS** (plus for pleasure, minus for pain). The seven criteria are (acronym **PRRICED**): **P**urity, **R**ichness, **R**eliability, **I**ntensity, **C**ertainty, **E**xtent, **D**uration. In this assessment "everyone is to count as one and no-one as more than one" (Bentham), so there is strict **EQUALITY**.

Quantative Pleasure

Bentham believed "pushpin is as good as poetry" (pushpin – a pub game = playing a slot machine in today's terms). Pleasure is purely **QUANTITATIVE** so we can't award more hedons to listening to Mozart or painting a picture or grasping philosophy. Mill, who was saved from mental breakdown by **WORDSWORTH**'s poetry, really objected to this. According to Bentham, we can compare a small child's delight in a new toy with someone else's delight in a new girlfriend. A **PIG** enjoying a good wallow is of more value than **SOCRATES** having a sightly sad think. Hence "*the pig philosophy*" (Thomas **CARLYLE**).

Pleasure Machines

JCC SMART (1973:18-21) asks us to imagine a pleasure machine where we can be wired up every day and passively enjoy every pleasure imaginable (note-addiction often operates like this as a kind of refuge in a supposed pleasure - like drink). **ALDOUS HUXLEY** wrote of a brave new world where people popped **SOMA** tablets to make them happy (there were 41m antidepressant prescriptions last year in the UK). Bentham can have no problems with this, but **MILL** saw happiness as a wider idea involving **ACTIVITY**, and realistic goals and expectations (closer to what my therapist might advise or what **ARISTOTLE** argues).

Strengths - Bentham

There is a **SIMPLICITY** in Bentham's calculation, and a radical **EQUALITY**. The **TELOS** of increasing human welfare is attractive and **COMMON SENSE**. His ideas drove **SOCIAL REFORM** – and he designed a more humane prison called a **PANOPTICON** – never built in the UK, but in Barcelona. There is a lack of snobbery in his classification of all pleasures as **EQUALLY VALID** – why should Mozart be thought better than Rap music (at least in giving pleasure)?

purity
remote-ness
reprod-ucability
intensity
certainty
extent
duration

HEDON-O-METER

JERRY BENTHAM'S 12 FRUIT SLURPER

Weaknesses

Bentham focuses only on **ACTIONS** so we have to keep on calculating (he doesn't allow us to have **RULES** to make life easier). He equates **PLEASURE** with **HAPPINESS** – but they don't seem to be equivalent (ask the athlete training for the Olympics whether the toil is pleasurable – but it doesn't mean a lack of contentment with training). We can always ask "you're going to the nightclub, but is that a **GOOD** idea?" (Good meaning "promoting your welfare"). Bentham implies pleasure is **MEASURABLE** (it isn't - how can we compare my hedon with yours?). Finally, he has no answer for Smart's **PLEASURE MACHINE** or Huxley's **SOMA** tablet (of course, they were writing two centuries later so even if his stuffed skeleton, residing in a cupboard in London University, could talk, we don't know what it would say!).

Key Quotes - Bentham

"Nature has placed mankind under two sovereign masters, pain and pleasure. It is for them to point out what we ought to do as well as determine what we should do". Jeremy Bentham, Principles of Morals

"In every human breast, self-regarding interest is predominant over social interest; each person's own individual interest over the interests of all other persons taken together". Jeremy Bentham, Book of Fallacies, p 392

"The community is a fictitious body," and it is but "the sum of the interests of the several members who compose it". Jeremy Bentham, Principles of Morals

"Prejudice apart, the game of pushpin is of equal value with the arts and sciences of music and poetry. If the game of pushpin furnishes more pleasure, it is more valuable than either". Jeremy Bentham, Principles of Morals

Mill's Rule Utilitarianism

Background

Following J.O. **URMSON** in 1953, most people describe Mill's form of Utilitarianism **WEAK** (because these aren't hard and fast rules, as with **KANT**), **RULE** (because he argues: follow social rules first, based on past experience of happiness) **UTILITARIANISM** (as it has the one fundamental principle at its core - maximise **UTILITY**). However, it is fundamentally wrong to call his utilitarianism **HEDONIC** (his view of happiness is closer to **ARISTOTLE** than **BENTHAM**) and **RELATIVISTIC** (as there's a non-negotiable **ABSOLUTE** at its core - **UTILITY**). If you read his essay carefully you will find he redefines happiness as he goes along, adding **SOCIAL RULES**, **JUSTICE** and **LIFETIME GOALS** to a list of necessary conditions, and even **PLEASURE** gets a special treatment as Mill distinguishes **HIGHER** and **LOWER** pleasures.

Key Terms

- **ACT UTILITARIANISM** (AU) measuring the utility of an individual act

- **RULE UTILITARIANISM** (RU) focusing on the rules which maximise social happiness

- **RIGHTS** legal obligations which maximise social utility

- **JUSTICE** certain principles, practices and rights which according to Mil guarantee social utility

- **QUALITATIVE PLEASURE** pleasure can be evaluated according to its social value as 'higher' (intellectual) and 'lower' (bodily)

Weak Rule Utilitarianism

The weak **RULE UTILITARIANISM** of John Stuart Mill (1806-73) is a **TELEOLOGICAL** (telos = goal) theory based on a definition of goodness as the **BALANCE** of happiness over misery.

This is a measurable, **EMPIRICAL** idea – measure the happiness effects of likely consequences – giving an **OBJECTIVE** measure of goodness.

Mill was against the **INTUITIONISTS** which he found too **SUBJECTIVE**. Mill argues that happiness is most likely to be maximised by generally following a set of **RULES** which society has found, by experience, maximise utility. But the rules can develop and in cases of moral dilemmas, we should revert to being **ACT UTILITARIANS** (so weak **RU**).

Structure of Thought

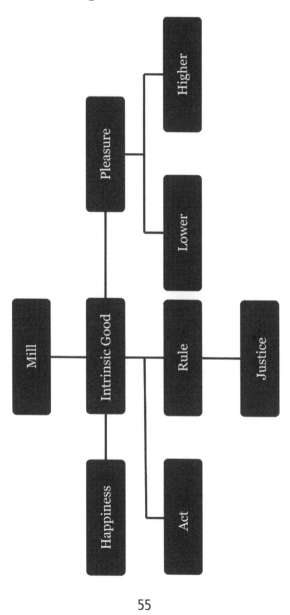

Mill & Bentham

Mill disliked three aspects of **BENTHAM**'s version.

1. The swinish implications of categorising all pleasures as of equal value – drinking beer v. listening to Mozart.

2. The emphasis on pleasure alone, as Mill was influenced by **ARISTOTLE**'s views on virtue (eg the importance of **SYMPATHY** for others).

3. The problem of **JUSTICE** and **RIGHTS** – how do we prevent one innocent person or group being sacrificed for the general happiness of the majority? So Mill devotes the last chapter of his essay to **JUSTICE**.

Mill on Happiness

Mill's definition of a happy life has three elements – pleasure (varied and rich) and absence of pain, **AUTONOMY** (the free choice of a life goal), and **ACTIVITY** (motivated by virtues like sympathy eg Mill used to hand out leaflets advising about contraception and campaigned for women's rights).

"**HAPPINESS** is not a life of rapture, but moments of such, in an existence with few and transitory pains, many and various pleasures, with a decided predominance of the **ACTIVE** over the passive, and having as a foundation of the whole, not to expect more from life than it is capable of bestowing". JS Mill, Utilitarianism

Higher and Lower Pleasures

Mill was saved from a nervous breakdown in his 20s by the **ROMANTIC MOVEMENT** eg Wordsworth's Lyrical Ballads. To him poetry was infinitely superior to **PUSHPIN** (a pub game). So "better to be Socrates dissatisfied than a fool satisfied".

The **LOWER** bodily pleasures (food, sex, drink, football) were of less value than the **HIGHER** pleasures (reading, listening to Mozart).

So Mill followed **ARISTOTLE** in seeing education as of vital importance (the supreme Greek value is **CONTEMPLATION** to gain wisdom). Only a person who'd experienced both could really judge the difference in **QUALITY** (so we say qualitative pleasure is superior to quantitative). He called those who hadn't experienced both "inferior beings". Does this make Mill a snob?

Rules

Mill has been called an "inconsistent utilitarian" (Alasdair MacIntyre) – because as his essay goes on he moves from **ACT** to **RULE** utilitarianism. We use generations of past experience to form rules, so we don't have to do a calculation to know whether murder or theft is "right". We inherit **BELIEFS** "and the beliefs which have thus come down are the **RULES** of morality for the multitude" (JS Mill). These are not fixed but "admit of continual improvement" – so not **ABSOLUTE**.

The **FIRST PRINCIPLE** is utility (or the Greatest Happiness Principle) and then **SECONDARY PRINCIPLES** (rules) come from this and are constantly evaluated against the first principle. Just as navigation is based on astronomy (Mill's own analogy) doesn't mean the sailor goes back to the stars every time – no he uses an **ALMANAC** – so, argues Mill, human beings follow a code book of rules passed down from previous generations as the best way to be happy.

But if the depth sounder disagrees with the chart datum (rules of past chart-plotter's experience) we revert to being act utilitarians (my analogy).

Justice

Bernard **WILLIAMS** argued that Utilitarianism violates our **MORAL INTEGRITY** by encouraging us to do things we would find repulsive – like his example of Jim who is invited to kill one Indian as an honoured guest in order to save nineteen others. This is the problem of **INJUSTICE** – the Southern States may have enjoyed lynching innocent people in the 1920s but this doesn't make it right.

Mill argues that unhappiness is caused by selfishness, by people "acting only for themselves", and that for a person to be happy they need "to cultivate a fellow feeling with the collective interests of mankind" and "in the **GOLDEN RULE** of Jesus we find the whole ethics of utility" (JS Mill).

So we need to defend personal **RIGHTS** and "Justice is a name for certain moral requirements, which, regarded collectively, stand higher in the scale of **SOCIAL UTILITY**, and are therefore of more paramount obligation, than any others", and " justice is a name for certain classes of **MORAL RULES**, which concern the essentials of human well-being". Rights, justice and the virtue of sympathy stop selfish self-interest destroying the happiness of others. So we escape the problem of Jim and the Indians.

Act or Rule?

LOUIS POJMAN argues (2006:111) that we can adopt a **MULTILEVEL** approach (this is what Mill seems to be doing in talking about **PRIMARY** and **SECONDARY** principles). So we can have three levels if we wish: rules of thumb to live by which generally maximise utility, a second set of rules for resolving conflicts between these, and a third process – an **ACT** utilitarian one, for assessing a difficult situation according to the Greatest Happiness Principle (eg lying to save a friend). But in this way philosophers like **J.O.URMSON** argue that **RULE** utilitarianism collapses into **ACT** utilitarianism. Mill might counter that we don't have the time, the wisdom, or the resources to keep calculating every action and this multilevel approach is therefore realistic and practical in a way that **KANT**'s deontology is unrealistic and impractical because it cannot handle **MORAL DILEMMAS**.

Strengths - Mill

RATIONALITY and **PRACTICALITY** Utilitarian ethics rests on a rational calculation of numbers of people whose pleasure or happiness is maximised. There is a clarity and simplicity to this.

EQUALITY is central. Bentham wrote "everyone is to count as one, and no-one as more than one". This radical idea implies that everyone has equal weight in the utility calculation.

MILL adds equal **RIGHTS**. Suppose, on an equal vote, you all vote for my dismissal (or even death) in line with maximising general happiness? Mill argues this sort of law would violate rights and such a society would not be one that we'd choose to live in - it would be miserable. "The utilitarian emphasis on impartiality must be a part of any defensible moral theory". (Rachels, 2006:114). Finally, utilitarianism takes account of the **FUTURE** – issues of climate change, potential future wars and famines all suggest we need an ethical theory that takes into account those yet unborn.

Weaknesses - Mill

MOTIVE, "why should I maximise pleasure or happiness?" We can't agree how to define pleasure or happiness. Bentham and Mill don't notice the difficulty of the concept of "pleasure" a fatal objection at the outset", Anscombe (1958:2). Then there is a difficulty in making me think of the interests (happiness) of others. Mill tries to bring "sympathy" in as a kind of virtue or psychological motive.

DISTRIBUTION problems emerge when I try to maximise **TOTAL** not **AVERAGE** happiness – eg low tax for the rich may raise the total but reduce average happiness, because the 10% super rich are much, much happier.

Finally **CONSEQUENCES** are hard to calculate if you don't have the omniscience of God. The **IRAQ WAR** may have seemed justifiable by the Greatest Happiness Principle - but looking with hindsight we might argue - better a Saddam Hussein in power than a million deaths?

Confusions - Mill

1. Was Mill an Act or Rule Utilitarian? He is sometimes described as a **WEAK RULE UTILITARIAN**. Mill believed that generally we should follow the rule as this reflects society's view of what maximises happiness from past social experience. But when a pressing utilitarian need arises we should break the rule and so become an act utilitarian.

2. "Mill took Bentham's view that happiness equates to pleasure". Sometimes Mill seems to argue this, but it's truer to say Mill's view is close to **ARISTOTLE**'s that happiness means "personal and social flourishing". So to Mill the individual cannot be happy

without the guarantee of certain rules and rights and clear goals to aim for.

3. "Utilitarianism ignores individual rights". Mill would vigorously deny this: rights are essential for the happy society and the happy society generally, with a sense of security, is essential for happy individuals. However, a Benthamite view of individual **ACT UTILITARIANISM** is subject to this criticism (as is US foreign policy which included Guantanamo Bay and Rendition), because many people's pleasure outweighs one or two people's pain (it's the **BALANCE** of pleasure over pain that matters morally).

4. "Utilitarianism is a form of egoism". Utilitarianism escapes this criticism for two reasons: there is an impartiality as "everyone to count as one" and secondly, because the virtue of **SYMPATHY** as a moral feeling is fundamental to my concern for your welfare.

Possible Exam Questions

1. Evaluate the view that utilitarianism does not provide a helpful way of solving moral dilemmas.

2. "The application of the greatest happiness principle in specific situations is not a sufficient guide to the good action". Discuss

3. "Pleasure is not quantifiable". Discuss

4. To what extent does utilitarian ethics provide a useful guide to issues surrounding business ethics?

Key Quotes - Mill

"It is better to be a human being dissatisfied than a pig satisfied; better Socrates dissatisfied than a fool satisfied". J.S.Mill, Utilitarianism

"Happiness is...moments of rapture...in an existence of few and transitory pains, many and various pleasures, with a predominance of the active over the passive..not to expect more from life than it is capable of bestowing". J.S. Mill, Utilitarianism

"Whatever we adopt as the fundamental principle of Morality refers to the first-order beliefs and practices about good and evil by means of which we guide our behaviour. For morality, we require subordinate principles to apply it by". (Fundamental principle = happiness is good, subordinate principles = rules) J.S. Mill, Utilitarianism

"By the improvement of education, the feeling of unity with our fellow-creatures shall be as deeply rooted in our character, as the horror of crime is in an ordinarily well brought up young person". (feeling of unity = sympathy) JS Mill, Utilitarianism

"To have a right, then, is, I conceive, to have something which society should defend me in possession of. If the objector asks why? I can give no other answer than general utility". J.S.Mill, Utilitarianism

"Justice is a name for certain moral requirements, which, regarded collectively, stand higher in the scale of social utility, than any others". J.S.Mill, Utilitarianism

"I account the justice which is grounded on utility to be the chief part, and incomparably the most sacred and binding part, of all morality." J.S.Mill, Utilitarianism

"Because our relation to the world is partly given by moral feelings, and by a sense of what we can or cannot "live with", to regard those feelings....as happening outside one's moral self is to lose one's moral identity; to lose one's integrity". (Bernard Williams, Utilitarianism For and Against pg 104)

"In the golden rule of Jesus of Nazareth we find the whole ethics of utility". JS Mill, Utilitarianism

Situation Ethics - Christian Relativism

Situation Ethics is a **NORMATIVE** theory (tells you what is right/wrong – what you ought to do), that is **TELEOLOGICAL** and **CONSEQUENTIALIST** (acts are right or wrong if they bring about good/ bad consequences, or can be seen as instrumentally good/bad) and **RELATIVIST** (there are no universal rules as actions depend on circumstances; there is just one general universal value – that of agape love). It is also **CHRISTIAN**, based on the principle of sacrificial love (**AGAPE**).

Introduction

Joseph Fletcher (1966) argued there are three approaches to ethics:

1. **LEGALISTIC** – someone who follows absolute rules and laws. Fletcher rejects this as it leads to **UNTHINKING OBEDIENCE** and needs elaborate systems of exceptions and compromises.

2. **ANTINOMIAN** – (nomos is Greek for law, so anti-law) or someone who rejects all rules and laws (Fletcher rejects this as it would lead to social **CHAOS**).

3. **SITUATIONAL** – Fletcher argues that each individual situation is different and absolute rules are too demanding and restrictive. Instead we should decide what is the most **LOVING** course of action (**AGAPE**). The Situationist has respect for laws and

tradition, but they are only guidelines to how to achieve this loving outcome, and thus they may be broken if the other course of action would result in more love.

However, Situation Ethics is not **FULLY** relativist: it has an absolute principle (love) that is non-negotiable.

Origins of Agape in the New Testament

William **TEMPLE** wrote "there is only one ultimate and invariable duty; and its formula is this: "thou shalt love thy neighbour as thyself" (1917:206). He went on: "what acts are right depends on circumstances" (1934:405). **FLETCHER** was inspired by Temple but also argues that love is the fundamental controlling norm. There is a case for arguing this from the New Testament.

- Love is the heart of God's **CHARACTER**. "God is love" (1 John 4:8). This echoes the Old Testament description of God as one "abounding in steadfast love and faithfulness" (Exodus, 34:8) in his revelation to Moses.

- Love is the fulfilling of the **LAW**. Love interprets the commandments and allows us sometimes to break them. In John 8 Jesus refuses to allow them to stone an adulterous woman in direct breach of Leviticus 20:10.

- Love is the heart of a controlling **PARABLE** of the Good Samaritan., (Luke 10). "Controlling" in the sense that Jesus' own sacrificial love mirrors that of the outsider who did all he could to help the victim, as priests and officials passed by, and so the parable 'controls' our interpretation of the entire mission of Christ.

- Love is Jesus' new **COMMAND** (John 13:34) - 'a new commandment I give to you to love one another as I have loved you".

- Sacrificial love (**AGAPE**) is the highest form of love; "Greater love has no man than this, that he lay down his life for his friends". John 15:13

- Love is also the supreme **VIRTUE** in the writings of Paul, with many characteristics (kindness, patience, forgiveness, positivity, hopefulness, perserverance), (1 Corinthians 13).

- Love is given to us by the **SPIRIT** of love, says Paul - the Holy Spirit. (Romans 5:5)

So although the Greeks had several words for love - friendship, family love, erotic love - the greatest moral value is given to **AGAPE**.

Four Working Principles

In Situation Ethics there are **FOUR WORKING PRINCIPLES** (Fletcher's own term).

1. **PRAGMATISM** – (what you propose must be practical – work in practice).

2. **RELATIVISM** – (there are no fixed, absolute rules – all decisions are relative to **AGAPE** love. If love demands that you steal food, then you should steal food. Notice this is special meaning of relativism - Fletcher calls his theory 'principled relativism' because every action is made relative to the one principle of agape love.

3. **POSITIVISM** – (Kant and Natural Law are based on reason as both theories argue reason can uncover the right course of action). Fletcher disagrees with this: you have to start with a **POSITIVE** choice or commitment – you need to want to do good. There is no rational answer to the question "why should I love?" We accept this norm by faith.

4. **PERSONALISM** – (people come first: you cannot sacrifice people to rules or laws)

Six Fundamental Principles

1. Nothing is good in itself except **LOVE** (it is the only thing that is absolutely good, the only thing with **INTRINSIC v**alue).

2. Jesus replaced the law with love or **AGAPE** ("The ruling norm of Christian decision is love, nothing else". Joseph Fletcher).

3. Love and **JUSTICE** are the same thing (if love is put into practice it can only result in fair treatment and fair distribution).

4. Love desires the good of **OTHERS** (it does not have favourites, but this doesn't mean we have to **LIKE** them).

5. Only the **END JUSTIFIES THE MEANS** (if an action causes harm, it is wrong. If good comes of it, it is right).

6. Love's decisions are made in each **SITUATION**.

Conscience

Fletcher argues conscience has many potential meanings:

- **THE VOICE OF GOD** - as in the writings of Cardinal John Henry Newman.

- **PRACTICAL REASON** or phronesis - one of two meanings in the writings of Thomas Aquinas.

- **AN INSTINCT** we are born with. Aquinas' other word for conscience is **SYNDERESIS,** meaning an innate conscience.

- **AS A VERB** - Fletcher rejects the idea of conscience as a 'faculty' and argues it is like a verb reflecting our actions in doing loving things: 'there is no conscience; 'conscience' is merely a word for our attempts to make decisions creatively, constructively, fittingly'. (1966:53)

Strengths - Situation Ethics

It takes **INDIVIDUALS** and their needs seriously. It's also **FLEXIBLE** and also allows us to make judgements in situations where two moral principles conflict. **LOVE** is an important value somewhat neglected by other theories, as the motive of sympathy in Mill's utilitarian ethics is not quite as strong as the **AGAPE** of Joseph Fletcher.

Weaknesses - Situation Ethics

LOVE is a very demanding value to place at the centre of your ethics - can anyone love sacrificially all the time? Mustn't we be selfish some of the time? Like all **CONSEQUENTIALIST** theories it's impossible to calculate into the future making this particular love calculation **IMPOSSIBLE**. William Barclay argues that Fletcher fails to realise the value of law - as an expression fo the collective wisdom of generations before us, so the moral law is a guide which we shouldn't throw away so easily. Law also defines the **FABRIC** of society.

Confusions

1. "Situation ethics is a form of relativism". Fletcher denies this as he argues it is 'principled relativism' - meaning that the supreme norm of love is applied to situations and made relative to need and circumstances. There is thus one absolute norm - **AGAPE.** This is not relativism in the sense of the denial of objective truth, it is relativism

in the sense of 'goodness is relative to the situation' (a relativism of application not of norms).

2. "Situation ethics is a religious ethic". It is true that **AGAPE** is a controlling norm of the **NEW TESTAMENT**. Also the parable of the Good Samaritan (Luke 10) appears to be a form of situationism 'go and do likewise', says Jesus, which seems to mean 'go and work out love in the situations you find yourself'. When Fletcher gave up Christianity he still argued that the non-Christian will equate goodness with an idea such as Aristotle's **EUDAIMONIA** (flourishing) whereas the Christian would always maintain **AGAPE** as the supreme norm. So there may be a difference there between atheistic situationism and religious forms.

3. "Jesus was a situationist". It is true that Jesus overthrows some elements of the **LEVITICAL CODE** of law such as stoning adulterers, the uncleanness of certain types of food (such as pork), the uncleanness of certain types of people (such as menstruating women). It is also true that the parable of the **GOOD SAMARITAN** promotes a situationist ethic. However, he also said "I came not to abolish the law but to fulfil the law" (Matthew 5:17). This implies that the fundamental principles of the law such as justice, truth and equality are perfectly fulfilled in Jesus, even if he rejects some of the ritualistic practices.

Possible Exam Questions

1. "Situation ethics is too demanding as a system of ethical decision-making". Discuss

2. "Goodness is only defined by asking - how is agape best served". Discuss

3. "Agape is not so much a religious idea as an equivalent to saying 'I want the best for you'". Discuss

4. Evaluate the extent to which situation ethics is individualistic and subjective.

Key Quotes - Situation Ethics

"Love alone is always good and right in every situation". Joseph Fletcher (Situation Ethics, 1966:69)

"Faith, hope and love abide, these three, but the greatest of all is love". 1 Corinthians 13:13

"God is love". 1 John 4:8

"A new commandment I give to you, that you love one another". John 13:34

"Love your neighbour as yourself". Jesus replied, 'Go and do likewise". Luke 10:27,28

"There can be and often is a conflict between law and love". Joseph Fletcher (1966:70)

"Too much law means the obliteration of the individual; too much individualism means a weakening of the law...there is a place for law as the encourager of morality". William Barclay, Ethics in a Permissive Society p189

In 1952 POPE PIUS XII called situation ethics "an individualistic and subjective appeal to the concrete circumstances of actions to justify decisions in opposition to the NATURAL LAW or God's revealed will'.

"High authority has held that a starving man should rather steal a loaf than die of hunger". William Temple (referring to Aquinas)

"Every moral act must be good or evil by reason of some circumstance". Thomas Aquinas (de Malo; Q2 A5c)

Euthanasia

Background

There have been numerous appeals to the law courts to get a **RIGHT** to euthanasia established in British law (see for example the Diane **PRETTY** case or Debbie **PURDY**). Interestingly, it is only the **SITUATION** ethicist who unambiguously defends Euthanasia (and then only for certain forms). In the UK we have an approach very similar to what a **WEAK RULE UTILITARIAN** would advocate: we follow the social rule (no euthanasia) but in certain cases we turn a blind eye and become **ACT UTILITARIANS**. For example doctors will increase a morphine dose with a dying patient's permission, having told them it will kill them (**VOLUNTARY ACTIVE EUTHANASIA**) - which corresponds also with the **PRINCIPLE** of **DOUBLE EFFECT** in **NATURAL LAW**. Because the **INTENTION**'s to relieve pain, this is neither illegal nor arguably immoral.

Definitions

- **EUTHANASIA** (Greek = good death) is the practice of ending life to reduce pain and suffering (so "mercy killing").

- **VOLUNTARY** euthanasia = when a patient's death is caused by another person eg doctor with the **EXPLICIT CONSENT** of the patient. The patient request must be **VOLUNTARY** (acting without coercion, pressure) **ENDURING** (lasts some time or is repeated over time) and **COMPETENT** (they have the mental capacity to choose). A variation on euthanasia is **PHYSICIAN-ASSISTED SUICIDE** – this differs from euthanasia as the doctor will help the patient to commit suicide (eg set up the apparatus), but the final act of killing is done by the patient.

- **NON-VOLUNTARY** euthanasia is done without the patient's consent, because they are not competent or able to give the consent (eg in a coma, on a life support machine). The doctor and/or the family may take the decision. A famous test case was that of **TONY BLAND** who was in a persistent vegetative state following the 1989 Hillsborough football disaster.

- **INVOLUNTARY** euthanasia is performed **AGAINST** the wishes of the patient. This is widely opposed and illegal in the UK.

Active or Passive

ACTIVE euthanasia is the direct and **DELIBERATE** killing of a patient.

PASSIVE euthanasia is when life-sustaining treatment is withdrawn or withheld.

This distinction may also be described as the difference between an **ACT** and an **OMISSION** (failing to act) and between **KILLING** and **ALLOWING TO DIE**. Some, such as James Rachels, argue there is no real difference – if anything passive euthanasia (withdrawal of treatment) is worse because it leads to a longer, drawn out death and so more suffering potentially. **DAME CICELY SAUNDERS** (who founded the hospice movement) argues that it is unnecessary for anyone to suffer a painful death with modern drugs. A counter-argument is that many doctors already hasten death (eg by doubling a morphine dose): under the doctrine of **DOUBLE EFFECT** (part of Natural Law theory), if the intention is to alleviate pain and a secondary effect to kill someone, the doctor is not guilty of any crime.

Legal Position

Until 1961 suicide was illegal in the UK. The **1961 SUICIDE ACT** legalised suicide, but made it illegal to assist someone.

The **NETHERLANDS** and **SWITZERLAND** allow voluntary euthanasia (**ACTIVE** and **PASSIVE**) and physician-assisted suicide. The **DIGNITAS** clinic in Switzerland helped 107 British people to die in 2010. **DR ANNE TURNER** (aged 66) was one such person in 2009 – subject of the docu-drama "A Short Stay in Switzerland". No-one has ever been prosecuted in the UK for helping a relative or friend go to Switzerland.

In 2010 Director of Public Prosecutions **KEIR STARMER** confirmed that relatives of people who kill themselves will not face prosecution as long as they do not maliciously encourage them and assist only a "clear settled and informed wish" to commit suicide. The move came after the Law Lords backed multiple sclerosis sufferer Debbie **PURDY**'s call for a policy statement on whether people who help someone commit suicide should be prosecuted.

Keir Starmer concluded: "There are **NO GUARANTEES** against prosecution and it is my job to ensure that the most vulnerable people are protected while at the same time giving enough information to those people like Mrs Purdy who want to be able to make informed decisions about what actions they may choose to take".

The **OREGON RULES** are another attempt to legalise assisted suicide by laying down conditions under which it will be allowed in US law.

Sanctity of Life - Bible

The Bible argues that life is a gift from God. Humans are created in the **IMAGE OF GOD** (Genesis 1:27) and the **INCARNATION** (God taking human form – John 1:14) shows the sacred value of human life. Human life is a **GIFT** or **LOAN** from God (Job 1:21 "The Lord gave and the Lord has taken away"). We should also show **RESPECT** for human life: "thou shalt not murder" (Exodus 20:13). We should also "choose life" (Deuteronomy 30). Finally, Christian love (**AGAPE**) is crucial (1 Corinthians 13 "the greatest value of all is love"). We should protect human life (the parable of the **GOOD SAMARITAN**) particularly as God gave his only son to redeem us (bring us back from sin and death) and give us the gift of "life in all its fullness".

Sanctity of Life - Ethical Theories

- The **NATURAL LAW** view argues that there is a **PRIMARY PRECEPT** to "preserve life" and views life as an **INTRINSIC** good. Euthanasia is therefore wrong and the Catholic Church forbids both active and passive euthanasia as "contrary to the dignity of the human person and the respect due to God, his creator" (Catechism of the Roman Catholic Church). However, the **DOCTRINE OF DOUBLE EFFECT** might accept the shortening of human life (eg if the intention is to relieve pain, secondary effect to kill) so long as it is only a **FORESEEN BUT UNINTENDED RESULT**. The Catholic Church also makes a distinction between **ORDINARY MEANS** (ordinary, usual medical treatments) and **EXTRAORDINARY MEANS** (treatments that are dangerous, a huge burden, or disproportionate). It is morally acceptable to stop extraordinary means, as "it is the refusal of over-zealous treatment".

- **ROMAN CATHOLIC** version of Natural law: "Discontinuing medical procedures that are burdensome, dangerous, extraordinary, or disproportionate to the expected outcome can be legitimate; it is the refusal of "over-zealous" treatment. Here one does not will to cause death; one's inability to impede it is merely accepted. The decisions should be made by the patient if he is competent and able or, if not, by those legally entitled to act for the patient, whose reasonable will and legitimate interests must always be respected." Catholic Catechism 2278

- **HUMANIST ARGUMENTS** Following Mill's **RULE** utilitarianism, we could argue that a. A general rule should be in place for social happiness prohibiting euthanasia (so the elderly don't feel under pressure or depressed people feel the temptation). But, b. In specific cases near the end of life doctor's using their discretion should hasten death. This is the present UK situation, which can be justified by rule utilitarian (non-Christian) arguments, giving a modified humanist sanctity of life view.

Quality of Life - Situation Ethics

JAMES RACHELS argues that the sanctity of life tradition places too much value on human life and there are times (eg with abortion and euthanasia) when this is unhelpful. He makes a distinction between **BIOLOGICAL LIFE** ("being alive" = functioning biological organism) and **BIOGRAPHICAL LIFE** ("having a life" = everything that makes us who we are). He says that what matters is biographical life and if this is already over (for example in a **PERSISTENT VEGETATIVE STATE = PVS**), then taking away biological life is acceptable.

PETER SINGER, a preference utilitarian, argues that the worth of human life varies (the value of human life is not a sacred gift but depends on its **QUALITY**). A low quality of life (judged by the patient) can justify them taking their life or justify someone else doing it for them.

SITUATION ETHICS would also take quality of life as more important than sanctity of life. **PERSONALISM** requires we take a case by case approach, and if someone is suffering in extreme discomfort, then **AGAPE** would dictate that we support their euthanasia. There may however be situations where someone is depressed, for example, where the most loving thing is to persuade them of a life worth living. **PRAGMATISM** demands a case by case and flexible approach. Joseph Fletcher was a himself a pioneer in bioethics and argued: "To bring this matter into the open practice of medicine would harmonise the civil law with medical morals, which must be concerned with the quality of life, not merely its quantity."

Autonomy

JOHN STUART MILL (On Liberty, 1859) argues that individuals should have full **AUTONOMY** (the freedom to make decisions without coercion) so long as it does not harm other people. Individuals cannot be compelled to do things for their own good – "over his own mind-body the individual is sovereign". Those who support voluntary euthanasia believe that personal autonomy and self-determination (choosing what happens to you) are crucial. Any competent adult should be able to decide on the time and manner of their death.

KANT assumes autonomy as one of his three key postulates (together with God and immortality). We are self-legislating, free moral beings.

However, he argued in an essay on suicide that suicide was self-contradictory as, if it was universalised, the human race would die out.

DIANE PRETTY argued in a court case in 2002 that Article 1 of the Human Rights Convention (the right to life) included the right to take one's own life. This autonomy argument was rejected by the court. She was paralysed by motor-neurone disease and requested permission for her husband to assist her to die.

Arguments Against Euthanasia

PALLIATIVE CARE – Dame Cicely Saunders argues that there is a better alternative for euthanasia in providing a pain-free death for terminally ill patients. The **HOSPICE** movement may be seen as an alternative, BUT this level of care is not available to everyone, is expensive and cannot fully relieve a patient's suffering (eg for someone who cannot breathe unassisted).

VOLUNTARY AND COMPETENT – some raise questions about voluntary euthanasia. Can the patient ever be free from coercion (eg relatives who want an inheritance or doctors who need to free up resources)? Is the patient likely to be competent (eg when under high doses of medication, or when depressed, or senile). Response would be that there are at least some clear cases when patients **ARE** clearly voluntary (not coerced) and competent. Guidelines such as Starmer's or the **OREGON RULES** require a certain time period of repeated requests to different people, which are then independently confirmed.

SLIPPERY SLOPE – this is the argument that once allowed, the outcome will be a process of a further decline in respect for human life and will end with the practice of non-voluntary euthanasia for the elderly seen as "unaffordable" by the working majority. A response might be that there is a clear difference between voluntary and non-voluntary euthanasia. Is there any evidence of a slippery slope in the US state of Oregon or Switzerland? The rules on assisted suicide are drawn up precisely to stop the slide into widespread disrespect for human life. Note this is an **EMPIRICAL, CONSEQUENTIALIST** argument about probabilities.

DOCTOR-PATIENT RELATIONSHIP – some argue that doctors have a duty to preserve life (the **HIPPOCRATIC OATH**). Euthanasia will undermine the trust between patient and doctor if there is a fear that they will seek to end their life. However, as with abortion, there will remain doctors opposed to euthanasia which a patient could always choose, and it is highly unlikely that GPs will have any say in the process of mercy killing.

Possible Exam Questions

1. Natural Law is superior to situation ethics in its treatment of issues surrounding euthanasia". Discuss

2. "Autonomy as an ideal is unrealistic. No-one is perfectly autonomous". Discuss with reference to the ethical issue of euthanasia.

3. "Sanctity of human life is the core principle of medical ethics". Discuss

4. "There is no moral difference between actively ending a life by euthanasia and omitting to treat the patient". Discuss

Key Quotes

"Euthanasia is contrary to the dignity of the human person and the respect due to God, His creator". Roman Catholic Catechism

"The Lord gave, the Lord takes away; blessed be the name of the Lord". Job 1:21

"God created man in His own image". Genesis 1:27

"God knit you together in your mother's womb". Psalm 139:6

"Discontinuing medical procedures that are burdensome, dangerous, or disproportionate to the expected outcome can be legitimate". Catechism

"Compare a severely defective human infant with a nonhuman animal, we will often find the non-human to have superior capacities". Peter Singer

"We see a life of permanent coma as in no way preferable to death". Jonathan Glover

"The ability to make complex judgements about benefit requires compassion, experience and an appreciation of the patient's viewpoint". British Medical Association

"Once the boundary is crossed it is hard to see how social and commercial pressures do not define the 'volunteers'." Alastair Campbell in Gill, R. ed Euthanasia and the Churches (Cassell, 1998 p 94)

'For all too many people there are good and reasonable grounds for the deepest despair. Where suffering is reasonably perceived to be unbearable, suicide can be morally right". James Gustafson Ethics from a Theocentric Perspective, (Chicago, 1984 p 214)

Business Ethics

Introduction

BUSINESS ETHICS is the critical examination of how people and institutions should behave in the world of commerce e.g. appropriate limits on self-interest, or (for firms) profits, when the actions of individuals or firms affect others. We may examine **CODES** which companies publish, or **BEHAVIOUR** of individuals – but also **CORPORATE CULTURE** (which may contradict the code) and responsibilities to the **ENVIRONMENT** and the developing world created by **GLOBALISATION** of markets and free trade between countries. We are asked to apply the Kantian idea of **UNIVERSALISED** duties and categoricals to business ethics, and utilitarian ideas of calculating net happiness or pleasure. according to **CONSEQUENCES**.

Key Terms

- **PROFIT MOTIVE** - the reward for risk-taking in maximising returns on any investment.

- **STAKEHOLDERS** - any parties affected by a business practice.

- **EXTERNALITIES** - costs or benefits external to the company – pollution is a negative externality.

- **GLOBALISATION** - the interconnection of economies , information and culture.

- **MULTINATIONALS** - companies trading in many countries.

Issues

Does the **PROFIT MOTIVE** conflict with ethical practice? Or does good ethics result in good business.

Should the regulation of business be left to **GOVERNMENTS**?

Ben and Jerry's has this **SOCIAL RESPONSIBILITY** statement at its heart: "to operate the company in a way that recognises the role business plays in the wider society and to find innovative ways to improve the life of the wider community". How widely is this view shared?

What happens when **STAKEHOLDER** interests conflict (eg sacking workers to raise shareholder returns?).

In a **GLOBALISED** world should we treat all workers the same irrespective of differences in national laws (think of safety regulations overseas)? Do **MULTINATIONALS** have too much power?

Stake-holders

A **STAKEHOLDER** is any individual or group who has a stake in the success or failure of a company. It includes **INTERNAL**

STAKEHOLDERS (managers, employees) and **EXTERNAL** (the local community, customers, shareholders, suppliers, local authorities, Government, other countries). For example, the existence of a Tesco store may mean local shopkeepers do better (if more people visit the town) or worse (if business is taken away).

Stakeholder theory suggest we should consider the interests of all stakeholders in the consequences of a decision.

Codes - Kant's Duty

Most companies have **CODES OF ETHICS** which lay out the rights of different groups and the responsibilities and values of the company. **ETHICAL INVESTORS** only invest in companies that fulfil certain criteria eg **ENVIRONMENTAL** responsibility, and **FAIR TRADE** for overseas workers.

ETHICAL CONSUMERS look for sustainable sources or organic produce. The April 2011 riots in **BRISTOL** against the Tesco local store show how different interests may clash – stakeholders such as local businesses/some customers v. large corporations/ other customers and employees. Does Tesco have an **ETHICAL DUTY** not to destroy local businesses, or a duty to its potential **EMPLOYEES** (jobs) and **CUSTOMERS** (lower prices)? Is there and **ABSOLUTE** principle we can find to judge between them? Most companies have ethics codes. Are they **CATEGORICALLY** followed? (Or just when it suits them?)

Cost/Benefit

COST/BENEFIT analysis is a business equivalent to **UTILITARIAN** ethics, as it seeks to weigh the benefits in money terms of a business decision against the cost. It suffers the same problem: the denial of **INDIVIDUAL RIGHTS** as a moral **ABSOLUTE**.

In the case of **FORD PINTO** (1970s) the cost of a **HUMAN LIFE** was weighed against the number of likely accidents and the cost of a **PRODUCT RECALL**. At $13 a car it was not worth the recall, they decided. But – they didn't calculate **CONSEQUENCES** correctly and valued **HUMAN LIFE** too cheaply – so ended up paying millions in compensation and having to **RECALL** the car anyway.

Unfortunately value has to be placed on a human life in traffic safety, **NHS** budgets etc – it's not economic to place a crash barrier alongside roads adjacent to remote reservoirs – so tragic accidents do occur (e.g in April 2011 four die in a car plunging into a reservoir in Wales).

If environmental costs are too high, will companies pay them or relocate their business?

Externalities

EXTERNALITIES are costs paid (eg pollution) or benefits enjoyed (eg flowers in a roundabout) by someone external to the firm.

Traditionally Governments have taxed and regulated firms to make them comply with their ethical duties: **THE TEN HOURS ACT** (1847 restricts child labour to 10 hrs a day), the **CLEAN AIR ACT** (1956 restricts carbon emissions), the **HEALTH AND SAFETY ACT** (1974 – improved safety standards and penalised non-compliance), the **SEX DISCRIMINATION ACT** (1975 – Equal Pay and opportunity for women).

MILTON FRIEDMAN (economist) argues that companies have a duty only to their shareholders (ie profits) – it is for society to set the other ethical rules. But examples such as **ENRON**, the US energy company that went bankrupt in 2003 after massive fraud, indicate that laws are never enough – individuals need to take **RESPONSIBILITY**.

As environmental regulation increases the cost to companies rises. Yet the USA has still not signed up to immediate carbon emission reduction despite the 1996 **KYOTO** protocol and the **COPENHAGEN** (2008)and **DURBAN** (2011) summits. Although China, Russia and America signed the Durban agreement, this only committed countries to define a future treaty by 2015, which will be binding in 2020.Once again immediate action has been postponed. US Senator Jim Inhofe, who has called climate change "the greatest hoax every perpetrated on the American people", applauded the "complete collapse of the global warming movement and the Kyoto protocol".

Rights

ABSOLUTISTS (eg Kantians) argue for universal human rights that apply everywhere for all time – including workers and communities in third world countries.

Because **GLOBALISATION** includes the free flow of **CAPITAL** to least cost countries, this can include those with corrupt governments or lax health and safety laws. Union Carbide (US firm) plant in **BHOPAL** (1986, India) and **TRAFIGURA** oil waste disposal (2008, Ivory Coast, hydrogen sulphide) illustrate how thousands can die (Bhopal – mustard gas) or go sick (Trafigura) when companies pursue least cost choices to boost **PROFIT**.
Worker and community rights often seem to take second place to **SHAREHOLDER** interests.

Individuals

Individual workers may become **WHISTLEBLOWERS** and expose fraud, corruption, lax standards etc. The RBS sacked their finance director who "didn't fit in" = opposed their lending policy before the **GLOBAL FINANCIAL CRISIS**.

UK banks were 24 hours from collapse in 2008 before a Government rescue plan, in taking on their bad debts. The rescue of **ROYAL BANK OF SCOTLAND** cost £43bn. But in the **EUROZONE** crisis countries act like individuals, with David Cameron vetoing a recent treaty change because of Britain's **NATIONAL INTEREST**. Is there such an idea as **COLLECTIVE** (European) interest?

Individual **CONSCIENCE** may serve the **public good,** but at the cost of their own **SELF-INTEREST** (they're fired). Kantian ethics may help us cling to **ABSOLUTES**, but Utilitarian ethics tends to make us pragmatists as at the **NORMATIVE** level we lie or stay silent to serve a **COLLECTIVE** interest (and we may not have enough sympathy with outsiders to care).

However **ENRON**'s collapse in 2003 brought down auditor **ARTHUR ANDERSEN** as it was implicated in the financial fraud which covered up huge debts, and affected shareholders, employees and pensioners. Sometimes **SHORT-TERMISM** in the utilitarian calculation can have terrible long-term consequences, and the courage of **ERIN BROKOVITCH** in exposing the toxic leaks of **PACIFIC GAS** in an American town shows how a Kantian sense of duty may have much to teach us in Business affairs, even though it can be risky for an individual to take on powerful corporations.There was one Enron whistleblower - Vice-President Sherron Watkins - but she only blew as far as Chairman Ken Lay.

Future Generations

One of the puzzles of ethics is how we account for the interests of future generations and animals, plants, etc. Both **KANTIAN** and **UTILITARIAN** ethics are traditionally weak on environmental issues (Kant stresses rational autonomous beings as having moral worth, not animals, and utilitarianism sees the environment as having only **INSTRUMENTAL** goodness as a means to human happiness. This may suffer from the problem of **SHORT-TERMISM)**.

UTILITARIANISM however can arguably do better because the long term happiness of the human race is clearly one factor to consider – but how do we know how many people to add in to the calculation? How do we assess the environmental effect of the plastic bag "island" the size of Texas which exists in the central vortex of the **PACIFIC** ocean currents? **SUSTAINABLE DEVELOPMENT** is a new idea – and **CHRISTIAN ETHICS** has arguably suffered from an emphasis on **DOMINION** (Genesis 1:26) = exploit, rather than **STEWARDSHIP** = care for the environment.

Can we provide incentives to this generation to protect future rights of the unborn?

Globalisation

Globalisation is the **INTERCONNECTION** of markets, technology and information across the world. There are said to be five global brands: Nike, Coca-Cola, McDonalds, Levis. However globalisation brings the risk that large companies dominate the political agenda working in their own interest, and also force wages down for third world suppliers. For example, multinationals fund **PRESIDENTIAL** campaigns and the oil industry lobbies ceaselessly to stop any rise in **OIL PRICES** and even, it has been alleged, the development of alternative energy sources.

The economist Amartya Sen has argued that the central issue is "the **UNEQUAL SHARING** in the benefits of globalisation" – that the poor receive an unequal gain from any wealth created. Put another way, less developed countries are exploited for cheap labour in the global market place (compare **WAGES PER HOUR** in China and the UK for example).

Finally there is the question of **REGULATION**. Do multinationals export lax safety standards and poor environmental disciplines to the third world? The examples of **BHOPAL** (1984) and **TRAFIGURA*** (2007) are not encouraging. And could any government have stopped a deregulated world banking system bringing the world economy to the brink of collapse in the crisis of 2008? Short-term profit and excessive **RISK-TAKING** in property lending led to the accumulation of huge debts so that Royal Bank of Scotland was only saved from bankruptcy by a £43bn cash injection by the UK Government.

Are multinationals beyond state regulation? Do they have too much power? What incentive do they have to be ethical?

* In 2007 Trafigura established a foundation to promote environmental concern, rural development programmes and health programmes in the counties where it operated. So far $ 14.5 m dollars has been donated to 36 projects. It is now seeking to create "a lasting, sustainable model for corporate philanthropy", perhaps trying to counteract the bad publicity generated by the waste dumping scandal.

Possible Exam Questions

1. "Kantian ethic of duty is superior to the utilitarian ethic of happiness in dealing with difficult business decisions". Discuss

2. "Corporate social responsibility is ethical window-dressing to cover their greed". Discuss

3. Evaluate the view that capitalism will always exploit human beings in the pursuit of profit.

4. "Globalisation widens the exploitation of human beings by reducing the need for ethically valid regulation of business behaviour". Discuss

Key Quotes

'Corporate executives do not have responsibilities in their business activities, other than to make as much money as possible for their shareholders" Milton Friedman

"Good employees are good people". Robert Solomon

"The following duties bind the employer: not to look upon their work people as their slaves, but to respect in every man his dignity as a person ennobled by Christian character". Rerum Novarum 1891(p 20)

"It matters that the prevailing ethos of a company brings together corporate purpose and personal values". Cardinal Vincent Nichols

'Serving the public and taking care of own's own employees are not an afterthought of business, but rather its very essence". Robert Solomon

'It is hard to separate businesses being ethical for its own sake with the fact that being ethical might be good for business". Wilcockson and Wilkinson OCR Religious Studies (Hodder, 2016)

'The solidarity that binds all men together as members of a common family make it impossible for wealthy nations to look with indifference upon the hunger, misery and poverty of other nations". Pope John XXIII.

"The natural environment is a collective good and the responsibility of everyone". Pope Francis

"Man should not consider his material possessions as his own, but as common to all, so as to share them without hesitation when others are in need." Thomas Aquinas (ST II-II, Q46, A2)

"The rights and duties of the employers, as compared with the rights and duties of the employed, ought to be the subject of careful consideration." Rerum Novarum 1891 (p 58)

Ethics in Year 2 (Spec. sections 4-6)

The Year 1 specification (assuming we follow it sequentially - sections 1-3) introduced **DEONTOLOGICAL** and **TELEOLOGICAL** ethics and asked the question: to what extent is ethics **ABSOLUTE** or **RELATIVE**? We then applied the **NORMATIVE** ethical theories of Situation Ethics and Natural Law to euthanasia, and Kantian Ethics and Utilitarianism to business ethics.

In Year 2 (sections 4-6 of the specification), the theories are now retained and a number of new issues considered in the nature and origin of **CONSCIENCE** (section 5). To deontology and teleology we add a study of the foundation of ethics **- META-ETHICS** (section 4), which includes the study of ethical meaning of the words "good' or "bad".

SEXUAL ETHICS (Section 6) is added as an applied issue (homosexuality, sex before marriage, and adultery). The specification asks us to consider,

"How the study of ethics has, over time, influenced and been influenced by developments in religious beliefs and practices, societal norms and normative theories". OCR H573 Specification

Both our **DEONTOLOGICAL THEORIES** (Kant and Natural Law - though Natural Law isn't pure deontology as it has a teleological aspect in the rational goals we pursue as human beings) and our **TELEOLOGICAL THEORIES** (Utilitarianism and Situation Ethics) are applied to issues surrounding **SEXUAL ETHICS**. Notice the following requirements to understand:

- traditional religious beliefs and practices (from any religious perspectives) regarding these areas of sexual ethics - for example as formed in Catholic **NATURAL LAW** theory and Papal Encyclicals (circulated letters) such as Humanae Vitae (1968)

- how these beliefs and practices have changed over time, including:

  o key teachings influencing these beliefs and practices
  o the ideas of religious figures and institutions

- the impact of **SECULARISM** (see also Christian Thought, paper 3, section 5) on these areas of sexual ethics

Notice that the work of **SIGMUND FREUD** on the unconscious and the **OEDIPUS COMPLEX** may also be relevant here (see section on Conscience). Together with **RICHARD DAWKINS** these are figures in our syllabus who form a basis for considering a secular worldview.

Key Terms

- **META-ETHICS** - concerns the nature and meaning of the words good and right. A key question in meta-ethics is: "Is goodness **OBJECTIVE** (linked to moral facts in the world) or **SUBJECTIVE** (up to me)?"

- **CONSCIENCE** - may come from **GOD**, our **UPBRINGING** or a process of **REASON**. "Where does conscience come from and how does it operate?" **PSYCHOLOGY** merges with philosophy here.

- **INTRINSIC THEORIES OF VALUE** - see something as good-in-itself. Does the pleasure for example have intrinsic value?

- **INSTRUMENTAL THEORIES OF VALUE** - see goodness relative to some end, such as human happiness. But in the debates within ethics, what do **DEONTOLOGISTS** like Kant or **TELEOLOGISTS** like Joseph Fletcher or JS Mill have to say about sexual ethics?

The Ethics Toolkit Revisited

The study of ethical theories so far has equipped us with a toolkit which we can use to assess any ethical issue. In this toolkit we derive insights from different theories.

KANT has given us the **PRINCIPLE OF UNIVERSALISABILITY**, a method of reasoning implying **CONSISTENCY** and a neutral point of view, and **PERSONAL AUTONOMY**, that places human choice and reason as a central ethical concern.

AQUINAS has given us the **PRINCIPLE OF NATURAL RATIONAL PURPOSE:** the idea of an order of being which is appropriate to our unique rational natures. The ultimate **TELOS** is **EUDAIMONIA** – well-being or personal and social flourishing.

UTILITARIANS have given us the **GREATEST HAPPINESS PRINCIPLE** and the **LEAST HARM PRINCIPLE**: the idea that we should always assess consequences in the light of an empirical calculation of the balance of happiness over misery, pleasure over pain or **WELFARE** over harm. In Economics we talk of **COST/BENEFIT** analysis.

RELATIVISTS encourage us to consider the **PRINCIPLE OF CULTURAL DIVERSITY** and to be humble in the face of claims that our own culture is objectively superior. All theories are to some extent children of their times.

Theories overlap to some extent and may not be as opposed as we sometimes think. For example, all of them discuss and claim for themselves the **GOLDEN RULE** "Do to others as you would have them do to you", Matthew 7:18 (is this therefore a good example of a universal ethical **ABSOLUTE**?).

All appeal to **VIRTUE** or character traits (**MILL** appeals to sympathy, **KANT** to dutifulness, **FLETCHER** to love, **AQUINAS** to practical wisdom and the Christian virtues of I Corinthians 13, faith, hope and love).

All theories have a **TELEOLOGICAL** aspect. Kant for example considers consequences in so far as he asks us to universalise the consequences of everyone doing what I do. He also envisages a goal, the **SUMMUM BONUM** which is similar in some ways to Aristotle's **EUDAIMONIA**.

Moreover, Aquinas' **NATURAL LAW** is best described as "a deontological theory arising out of a Greek teleological worldview" where the good is defined by the rational end (**TELOS**).

Meta-Ethics

Background

META-ETHICS means "beyond ethics" (metaphysics - beyond physics). Rather than asking how we derive moral principles like "do not kill", meta-ethics asks us to consider what moral statements mean and what the **FOUNDATION** of ethics might be. Here are some of the key issues:

Is there an **OBJECTIVE** principle we can appeal to resolve moral disputes? Or are we inevitably in a world of **RELATIVISM** and **SUBJECTIVISM** where such questions are "up to me"?

When I say "stealing is wrong" am I describing some **FACTS** about the world which we can look at, examine, appeal to, or am I only stating an opinion or expressing a feeling?

Is moral **LANGUAGE** a special type of language where words like "good" and "ought" mean something quite specific and different from other uses of, for example, "good" (**DESCRIPTIVE** meanings, rather than **PRESCRIPTIVE** or action-guiding, moral meanings)? Is the meaning of good in the sentence "that's a good painting" (which applies criteria such as composition, use of colour etc) different from the moral use "good boy!", (praising the child and saying effectively - keep on behaving like that")?

Specification

NATURALISM (the belief that values can be defined in terms of some natural property in the world) and its application to **ABSOLUTISM**
INTUITIONISM (the belief that basic moral truths are indefinable but self-evident) and its application to the term good
EMOTIVISM (the belief that ethical terms evince approval or disapproval) and its application to **RELATIVISM**

Key Terms

- **ANALYTIC** - true by definition "all bachelors are unmarried".

- **SYNTHETIC** - true by observation "John is a bachelor".

- **A PRIORI** - before experience.

- **A POSTERIORI** - after experience.

- **COGNITIVISM** - moral facts can be known objectively as **TRUE** or **FALSE**.

- **NATURALISM** - moral goodness is a feature of the natural world, and so an **A POSTERIORI** fact.

- **NATURALISTIC FALLACY** - you cannot move without supplying a missing **PREMISE** from a descriptive statement such as "kindness causes pleasure" to a moral statement "kindness is good".

Note: **HUME** was himself a father of the utilitarian **NATURALISTS** as he argued that morality derives from the natural feeling of sympathy. He never said "you cannot move from an 'ought' to an 'is'", but only that if we do so, we must provide a missing **PREMISE** with a value-statement in it, such as "pleasure is good as it leads to a happy life". However Hume's theory of language is developed by **AJ AYER** in the theory of **EMOTIVISM** - a non-naturalist theory of how moral language works and Hume never supplied the missing premise himself (but implies that the origin of morality is found in naturalistic sentiments of approval).

Cognitive or Non-Cognitive

COGNITIVISTS believe goodness can be known as an **OBJECTIVE** feature of the world - where "objective" means "out there where it can be analysed, measured, and assessed". So cognitivism says "ethical statements can be proved true or false".

Something about our reason allows us to do this either by making some measurement (for example of happiness as the utilitarians do) or working out a principle **A PRIORI**, before experience, as Kant argues we do in deriving the **CATEGORICAL IMPERATIVE**.

NON-COGNITIVISTS argue there is no objective, factual basis for morality - it is subjective and up to me to determine. Ethical statements don't have **TRUTH VALUE** - they are empirically unprovable. Put another way - **NON-COGNITIVISTS** can say 'there is no such thing as a moral fact" such as the fact of pleasure or pain identified by Utilitarians.

Structure of Thought

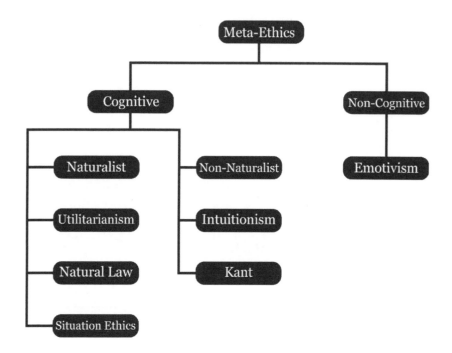

The **NATURALISTS** argue we can resolve this issue empirically (**A POSTERIORI** - from experience) by looking at some observable feature of an action - a fact such as "it causes pain" (a utilitarian concern) or "it fulfils the natural rational purpose of human beings" (the **EUDAIMONIA** or goal of flourishing of **NATURAL LAW**).

NON-NATURALISTS argue either that the truth is a priori (Kant for example, even though he argues for **COGNITIVISM**) or that there are simply no facts which we can identify as moral facts – so that making a moral statement adds nothing to what we already know from a factual basis. This form of **NON-COGNITIVIST** non-naturalism is called **EMOTIVISM**.

The Naturalistic Fallacy

Developing a point made by David Hume, philosophers like **GE MOORE** have argued that when we move from a description about the real world to a moral statement we make a leap from a naturalistic statement to a **PRESCRIPTIVE** statement (one with ought in it). This prescription is doing something different.   What we often fail to do is explain the missing link between a description and a prescription - and this leap from is to ought is what is known as the **NATURALISTIC FALLACY**. A.N. Prior (1949) explains the fallacy:

"Because some quality invariably accompanies the quality of goodness, this quality is identical with goodness. If, for example, it is believed that whatever is pleasant is good, or that whatever is good must be pleasant, or both, it is

committing the naturalistic fallacy to infer from this that goodness and pleasantness are the same quality. The naturalistic fallacy is the assumption that because the words 'good' and 'pleasant' necessarily describe the same objects, they must attribute the same quality to them". AN Prior (1949)

MOORE argued that goodness cannot be a **COMPLEX** analysable property of an action. For example a horse can be broken down into animal, mammal, four legs, hairy tail – a **COMPLEX** idea. Because goodness isn't a complex idea, it must be either a **SIMPLE**, indefinable quality or it doesn't refer to anything at all. Since ethics isn't an **ILLUSION**, goodness must consist in a simple **INDEFINABLE QUALITY**, like the colour yellow.

The Open Question

MOORE pointed out that the naturalistic fallacy, of implying that goodness was identical to some specific property such as pleasure, is susceptible to the **OPEN QUESTION** attack. Suppose I say "this ice cream causes me so much pleasure" and then say "ice cream is good!". The open question attack suggests I can always ask the question "it produces pleasure, but nonetheless, is it morally **GOOD**?"

If I can answer "no" to this point then I have proved that goodness is something independent of pleasure.

Moore's Intuitionism

Moore was a non-naturalist **COGNITIVIST** because he believed that goodness could not be defined by its natural properties, but that we know what we mean by good by a special intuition or perception (so **COGNITIVIST**, as goodness can be known as a shared experience).

Moore argues goodness is an **INDEFINABLE PROPERTY** of an action just as the colour yellow is a non-definable property of a lemon - we know what it is and that's the end of it. We can try and reduce yellowness to light waves but that doesn't precisely tell us what yellow is - yellow just is yellow, we know this by intuition. Notice this is a version of non-naturalism as goodness cannot be established as a fact of sense experience, but as a **NON-NATURALISTIC** perception.

Evaluation of Intuitionism

Moral intuitions are said to be like the **ANALYTIC** truths of Mathematics. But moral statements are more than just "true by definition". Peter Singer comments:

"Thus the intuitionists lost the one useful analogy to support the existence of a body of truths known by reason alone".

Intuitionists **CAN'T AGREE** what these moral goods are. So how can they be **SELF-EVIDENT**? Moreover, Moore's theory is also open to his own **OPEN QUESTION** attack on ethical **NATURALISM**: "that may be your intuition (eg genocide is okay), but is it **GOOD**?"

If intuitions are actually **CULTURAL CONSTRUCTS** as Freud suggests, then they cannot be **SELF-EVIDENT**.

Moore is arguing that moral truths are similar to **PLATO**'s ideal forms. John Maynard **KEYNES** once commented that "Moore could not distinguish love, and beauty and truth from the furniture", so enraptured was he by his idealised world of the forms.

Moore also confuses a complex thing (colour) for a simple thing (yellow). Goodness is in fact a **COMPLEX** idea, like **COLOUR** because it includes within it a whole class of principles we might describe as good (like colour includes, red, yellow, green, blue).

Moore has confused a general category (colour, goodness) for a specific quality of that category (yellowness, generosity).

Utilitarian Naturalists

Utilitarians are normative **NATURALISTS** because they argue that goodness is an observable feature of the natural world - part of our **A POSTERIORI** experience of pleasure and pain. So to work out what is good, we need to project into the future and balance the likely pain and pleasure of our choice. That which maximises happiness and minimises pain is good, and actions that do the opposite are bad.

Utilitarians quite openly commit the **NATURALISTIC FALLACY** (which they argue isn't a fallacy at all) arguing that it is obviously good to pursue happiness because that as a matter of fact is the goal that all humans are pursuing. They give a **TELEOLOGICAL** justification for goodness, just as **NATURAL LAW** theorists such as **AQUINAS** follow Aristotle in linking goodness to **HUMAN FLOURISHING**.

The philosopher **JOHN SEARLE** gives us another naturalist way out of the supposed fallacy. If I promise to pay you £500 then I am doing two things - I am agreeing to play the promising game which involves **OBLIGATION** to pay your money back, and I am accepting that part of the rules of the game, fixed by society, in that I can only break this promise if a large, overriding reason appears for doing so (for example, the money is stolen from me and I am bankrupt, so can't pay it back).

So the making of a promise is a **FACT** but because of the logical feature of promising - that I agree to it creates obligations for me - this allows us to move from a descriptive **IS** statement (Brian owes me £5) to a value **OUGHT** statement "you ought to keep your promise".

Ayer's Emotivism ("Expressivism")

A.J. Ayer (1910-1989) formed part of a school of linguistic philosophy called **LOGICAL POSITIVISM** which had at its heart the **VERIFICATION PRINCIPLE**. Truth claims had to be verified true or false by sense-experience. His theory is a theory of **NON-COGNITIVISM** as he argues moral statements add no facts — just opinions which cannot be established true or false empirically. So moral truth cannot be **KNOWN** as objective fact.

> "*The fundamental ethical concepts are unanalysable inasmuch as there is no criterion by which to judge the validity of the judgements. They are mere pseudo-concepts. The presence of an ethical symbol adds nothing to its factual content. Thus if I say to someone 'You acted wrongly in stealing the money,' I am not stating anything more than if I had simply stated 'you stole the money'". Language, Truth and Logic (1971)*

This approach to moral language was a development of **HUME's FORK** - an argument about language developed by David Hume. Hume argued that statements about the real world were of two sorts - they were either analytic or synthetic: either **LOGICAL TRUTHS** or **STATEMENTS OF FACT**.

An analytic statement is true by definition (2 + 2 = 4), a **SYNTHETIC** statement true by experience. So "all bachelors are unmarried" is true by definition, whereas "John is a bachelor" is true by experience (John might be married so that would make the statement **EMPIRICALLY** false). As moral statements are neither **ANALYTIC** (they'd have nothing useful to say about the **REAL** world if they were) or **SYNTHETIC** (not **VERIFIABLE**) they are logically and empirically meaningless.

Ayer put the same point another way.

> "*The presence of an ethical symbol in a proposition adds nothing to its factual content". (1971:142).*

Ayer believed that problems arose when the **NATURALISTS**, such as the **UTILITARIANS** claimed an empirical basis for goodness in the balance of pleasure over pain. What happens when one person's pleasure is another person's pain? Consider that someone steals your wallet. To you, stealing is wrong because it causes you pain. To the thief, stealing is good, because it gives her money to buy food, and she's starving. Stealing appears to be **BOTH** right and wrong at the same time.

This contradictory result indicates there can be no **FACT** of morality – just an **OPINION**.

> *"It is not self-contradictory to say some pleasant things are not good, or that some bad things are desired". (Ayer, 1971:139)*

Ayer means by this that if I say "you were wrong to steal" there is no additional **FACT** introduced by the word "wrong" - only an **EXPRESSION** of a feeling of disapproval. Note he argues the word **GOOD** is not describing a feeling but, in is own words "**EVINCING**" a feeling - like letting out a squeal if you hit your thumb, **"OUCH"**!.

> *"Stealing money is wrong expresses no proposition which can be either true or false. It's as if I had written "stealing money!!!" where the exclamation marks show a special sort of moral disapproval". A.J. Ayer*

Evaluation - Ayer

Ayer's view seems to be a radical **SUBJECTIVISM** suggesting morality is just "up to me". It seems to strengthen the case for **RELATIVISM** that

115

makes moral debate impossible and disagreements insoluble, even though this is not a theory of **NORMS** but of **MEANING**.

Ayer's view is based on a **FALLACY**. Ludwig Wittgenstein demonstrated that language is part of a game we play with shared rules. **MORAL** language is neither analytic nor synthetic but rather, **PRESCRIPTIVE** as Hare suggests (below). Ayer has committed a fallacy like saying "the world is either square or flat". It's neither.

According to Alasdair **MACINTYRE** in After Virtue, emotivism obliterates the distinction between manipulative and non-manipulative behaviour. There is no longer such an idea as a **VALID REASON**. Moral discourse is simply about manipulating you to adopt my point of view.

Absolutism & Relativism

Both these are ambiguous ideas. Relativism has three meanings: **PARTICULAR** to culture, **CONSEQUENTIALIST** and **SUBJECTIVE** (up to me).

Absolutism has three meanings which are the opposite: **UNIVERSAL** (applies everywhere and for all time), **NON-CONSEQUENTIALIST** and **OBJECTIVE**.

Theories may not be consistently absolute in all three meanings as the table overleaf demonstrates.

Theory	Universal	Non-consequentialist	Objective
Utilitarianism	YES, it claims we all experience pleasure and pain	NO, as goodness is always relative to maximising happiness	YES, as pleasure and happiness are measurable otherwise they couldn't be maximised
Situation Ethics	YES, as we can all understand and live by agape love	NO, as we maximise the value of love	YES, as there is a measurable test for ethical goodness
Kantian Ethics	YES, as we can all universalise a priori	YES, as categorical absolute rules are created	YES, as the Moral Law exists as an objective truth
Natural Law	YES, as we all share one rational human nature	NO, as secondary precepts are applications of reason and never absolute	YES, the world and human nature is set up in certain way - and operates by objective laws

We may therefore conclude that only **KANTIAN** ethics is absolute in all three possible meanings. The other theories have an **ABSOLUTE** element - they have a non-negotiable principle at their heart. That's why Joseph Fletcher calls his theory ~ **PRINCIPLED RELATIVISM** (the absolute principle is **AGAPE**) made relative always to consequences - the second meaning of relativism given earlier.

Is **EMOTIVISM** a form of **RELATIVISM**? It is a meta-ethical theory, not a normative one, and so in one sense the question is a **CATEGORY MISTAKE** as the term can only be applied to the derivation of norms.

However, in stressing the absence of **MORAL FACTS** and arguing that moral statements are neither analytic nor synthetic, and therefore meaningless in empirical terms, emotivism does appear to reinforce **SUBJECTIVISM** (our first meaning of relativism).

C.L. Stevenson's Emotivism

Stevenson argued that three criteria must be fulfilled when we use the word "good":

1. We must be able to agree that the action is good.

2. The action must have a **MAGNETISM** - we must want to do it, and feel an **INTEREST** in its being done.

3. The action cannot be verified empirically by appeal to facts.

So moral language has an **EMOTIVE** meaning and a **PERSUASIVE** meaning – we are encouraging others to share our attitude. This is why we bother to **ARGUE** about ethics, whereas on questions of taste we "agree to differ".

> "Good has an emotive meaning...when a person morally approves of something, he experiences a rich feeling of security when it prospers and is indignant or shocked when it doesn't". C.L .Stevenson.

R.M.Hare's Prescriptivism

R.M. Hare (1919-2002) argued that moral judgements have an **EMOTIVE** and a **PRESCRIPTIVE** meaning. This implicitly disagrees with the view of **HUME** and **AYER** who argue that meaningful statements are either analytic (true by definition) or synthetic (true by experience.)

Prescriptions are forms of **IMPERATIVE**: "you oughtn't steal" is equivalent to saying "**DON'T STEAL!**".

Hare agrees that you cannot derive a **PRESCRIPTION** such as "run!" from a description "there's a bull over there!" as there is a **SUBJECTIVE** element (I may choose to walk calmly or stand and wave my red rag). I am free to judge, hence the title of his book **FREEDOM** and **REASON**.

Hare follows **KANT** (even though Hare is a preference utilitarian) in arguing that **REASONABLENESS** lies in the **UNIVERSALISABILITY** of moral statements. Anyone who uses terms like "right" and "ought" are **LOGICALLY COMMITTED** to the idea that any action in relevantly similar circumstances is also wrong (see Kant's first formula of the **CATEGORICAL IMPERATIVE**).

So if Nazis say "Jews must be killed", they must also judge that if, say it turns out that they are of Jewish origin, then they too must be killed. Only a **FANATIC** would say this.

Hare argues for the importance of **MORAL PRINCIPLES** rather than **RULES**. It is like learning to drive a car:

"The good driver is one whose actions are so exactly governed by principles which have become a habit with him, that he normally does not have to think what to do. But all road conditions are various, and therefore it is unwise to let all one's driving become a matter of habit". (Hare, Language of Morals, page 63)

MORAL PROGRESS

Evaluation - Prescriptivism

Hare is still denying there are **OBJECTIVE** moral truths. We are free to choose our own principles and determine our actions according to our desires and preferences – there is no objective right and wrong independent of our choosing, but then having chosen, we must be able to universalise it. As a **NON-NATURALIST** he avoids reference to any final **TELOS** such as human flourishing.

Philippa **FOOT** criticised Hare in her lecture in 1958 ("Moral Beliefs") for allowing terribly immoral acts (and people) to be called "moral" simply because they are **CONSISTENT**. We cannot avoid approving the statement "If I was a murderer, I would want to be dead too if I support the death penalty". Prescriptivism cannot help justifying **FANATICISM**.

In his later book **MORAL THINKING** Hare brings together **PRESCRIPTIVISM** and his version of **PREFERENCE UTILITARIANISM**. To prescribe a moral action is to universalise that action – in universalising

"I must take into account all the ideals and preferences held by all those who will be affected and I cannot give any weight to my own ideals. The ultimate effect of this application of universalisability is that a moral judgement must ultimately be based on the maximum possible satisfaction of the preferences of all those affected by it". (Peter Singer)

Hare's pupil **PETER SINGER** builds on this idea to give prescriptivism an **OBJECTIVE** basis in his own version of preference utilitarianism. We are asked to universalise from a neutral, universal viewpoint.

So in the end prescriptivism escapes the charge of being another form of radical **SUBJECTIVISM**.

The Legacy of David Hume

David Hume argued that morality was a matter of acting on desires and feelings. Moral reasoning really reduces to the question "what do I want?" – it remains radically **SUBJECTIVE**. If Hume is right, there is no answer to the question "why should I be moral?" or "why should I be benevolent?". If I don't want to be moral, that seems to be the end of the argument.

J.L. MACKIE (Inventing Right and Wrong,1977) argues that the common view of moral language implies that there are some objective moral facts in the universe. But this view is a **MISTAKE**. There are no moral facts. We can only base our moral judgements on **FEELINGS** and **DESIRES**.

The **INTUITIONISTS** (G.E. Moore, H.A. Prichard, W.D. Ross) are arguing that there are **MORAL FACTS** but that we can only know them **NON-NATURALLY** as internal intuitions. This seems to be an attempt to have our cake and eat it.

R.M. HARE does have an answer to the question "why should I be moral?" At least in his later book **MORAL THINKING**, Hare argues that people are more likely to be happy if they follow universal **PRESCRIPTIVISM** and reason from a viewpoint that takes into account the interests and preferences of all people affected by my decision. However, this is an appeal to **SELF-INTEREST** – Hare is still an **SUBJECTIVIST**.

NATURAL LAW suggests a **NATURALIST** reason for being moral : we are moral to achieve personal and social **FLOURISHING**. If we can share the insights of psychology and philosophy we can come to a shared (if still **RELATIVISTIC**, cultural) view of what will build the excellent life. Naturalism has undergone a resurgence in the twentieth century, led by Geoffrey **WARNOCK** (1971, The Object of Morality) and Alasdair **MACINTYRE** (1981, After Virtue).

More recent, subtler, attempts to escape **SUBJECTIVISM** are to be found in John **RAWLS'** A Theory of Justice, which asks us to assume the role of an avatar in a space ship, imagining we are in an **ORIGINAL POSITION** heading to a new world where we don't know our gender, intelligence, race, or circumstances. What rules would we formulate for this world? Rawls, like Hare, brings **KANT** back into the forefront of meta-ethical debate.

Key Confusions to Avoid

1. "Utilitarianism is a meta-ethical theory". No, utilitarianism is a **NORMATIVE** theory that is built upon the meta-ethical view that the foundation of morals is **NATURALISTIC** - out there to be observed in the world **A POSTERIORI** (by experience of pleasure and pain). Meta-ethics has nothing to say about exactly how **NORMS** (values of goodness) are derived.

2. "Normative ethics is more useful than meta-ethics". This old exam question has a central ambiguity - more useful for what and to whom? If you're facing a **MORAL DILEMMA**, meta-ethics has no use at all because it doesn't produce a structure of thought for deciding what to do.

3. "Meta-ethics is boring". This is because it is sometimes badly taught. Actually the structure of morality that builds from meta-ethical **FOUNDATIONS** to **NORMATIVE THEORY** to **PRACTICAL CONCLUSION** is a fascinating one, and we need to think long and hard about how we are to solve moral problems - both **GLOBAL** (war, famine, injustice, poverty, exploitation) and **PERSONAL** (euthanasia, sexual ethics) even though the specification is biased (as in western thought generally) towards the personal.

Possible Future Questions

1. "The meaning of the word 'good' is the defining question in the study of ethics". Discuss

2. Critically consider whether ethical terms such as good, bad, right and wrong have an objective factual basis that makes them true or false.

3. "Ethical statements are merely an expression of an emotion". Discuss

4. Evaluate the view that ethical statements are meaningless.

5. "People know what's right or wrong by a common sense intuition". Discuss

6. Critically contrast the views of intuitionists and emotivists on the origin and meaning of ethical statements.

Key Quotes - Meta-ethics

"That which is meant by "good" is the only simple object of thought which is peculiar to ethics". G.E. Moore

"As this ought expresses some new relation it is necessary that it should be observed and explained and at the same time that a reason be given". David Hume

"The use of "That is bad!" implies an appeal to an objective and impersonal standard in a way in which "I disapprove of this; do so as well!" does not. If

emotivism is true, moral language is seriously misleading". Alasdair MacIntyre

"Good serves only as an emotive sign expressing our attitude to something, and perhaps evoking similar attitudes in other persons". A.J. Ayer

"To ask whether I ought to do A in these circumstances is to ask whether or not I will that doing A in these circumstances should become a universal law". R.M. Hare

"We have an idea of good ends that morality serves. Even if we are deontologists, we still think that there is a point to morality, to do with better outcomes — truth-telling generally produces better outcomes than lying. These ends can be put into non-moral language in terms of happiness, flourishing, welfare, or equality". Louis Pojman

Suggested Reading

Moore, G.E. (1903) Principia Ethica, Chapter II (see peped.org/meta-ethics/extract)
Ayer, A.J. (1936) Language, Truth and Logic, London: Victor Gollancz, Chapter 6 (see peped.org/meta-ethics/extract)
Mackie, J.L. (1977) Ethics: Inventing Right and Wrong, London: Penguin Books, Part 1.3

Conscience

Issues

There are four major issues in a study of conscience.

- What is the **ORIGIN** of conscience: does it come from God, our upbringing or from reason?

- What is the relation between **MORALITY** and **GUILT** feelings? Is guilt a product of certain complexes, such as Freud's **OEDIPUS COMPLEX?**

- How does conscience **WORK**: is it a **MENTAL PROCESS** and so part of our **REASON**, a **FEELING**, or a **VOICE** in our heads (e.g. the voice of God?)?

- Can we go against our conscience and choose to reject it, in other words, is conscience **FALLIBLE** and so likely to make mistakes, or is it inerrant (incapable of error)? What is the relationship between conscience and human **WILL**?

Specification

Requires us to consider **FREUD**'s Psychological approach and **AQUINAS'** Theological Approach, to compare and critically evaluate these two theories. We are at liberty to contrast them with Eric **FROMM**,

BUTLER or **NEWMAN** or anyone else - the syllabus is open-ended about additional material. We do, however, need to compare and contrast them with philosophers/authors of a different persuasion - so these are included in this guide. Students need to decide which is most relevant to their own approach of critical analysis and evaluation of Aquinas and Freud.

The Psychology of Conscience - Freud

Background

ENLIGHTENMENT – believed in reason and measurement but also hypothesis tested **A POSTERIORI.** Freud shared this belief that science could probe the deepest unconscious recesses of the human mind and so contribute to the advancement of human welfare.

- **COPERNICUS** taught us that humans were not the centre of the universe.

- **DARWIN** taught us that humans were just another species of animal.

- **FREUD** taught us that humans were not rational actors, but rather are driven by unconscious, primitive, instinctual desires.

Key Terms

- **CATEGORICAL IMPERATIVE** unconditional demands of the superego whose violation produces guilt

- **CONSCIENCE** The part of human consciousness that guides moral decisions and equivalent to the superego

- **EGO** The part of the human mind that forms our idea of self and presents a coherent image to the outside world. The ego longs for a moral guide.

- **ID** The part of the human mind which processes passions and emotions. It is non-moral and is often in conflict with ego and superego.

- **SUPEREGO** The part of the human mind which regulates behaviour, formed in childhood by relationships with authority figures (father and mother) and by praise and blame.

- **REPRESSION** The suppression of our real emotions because they do not conform to ego-identity or are categorized as shameful by the superego.

- **EROS** The creative life-force which is also the mischief-maker as it encourages the ego to take risks and cross boundaries.

- **THANATOS** The death-instinct in conflict with eros, which appears in destructive patterns of behaviour (self-harm, aggression, and suicide).

- **UNCONSCIOUS** That part of the iceberg of the human mind which lies unseen but nonetheless influences and even controls behaviour.

- **LIBIDO** The sexual instinct which forms part of eros and is often repressed or overly controlled by the superego.

- **NEUROSIS** Mental illness which results from a failure to create a coherent and harmonious ego. Examples might be hysteria, obsessive-compulsive disorders (e.g. washing rituals) and phobias (e.g. spiders).

Structure of Thought

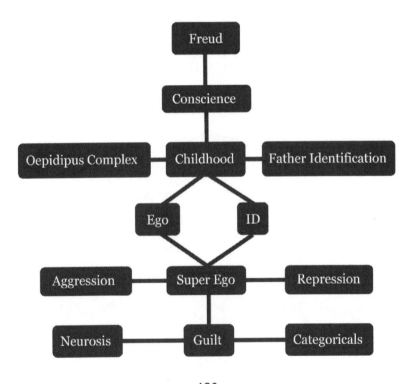

Freudian Revolution

Sigmund Freud (1856-1939) is the **FATHER OF PSYCHOANALYSIS** through his theories of how the conscious and unconscious mind develop and interact. He believed in the **ENLIGHTENMENT** assumption that science could understand all aspects of human behaviour by observing **A POSTERIORI** how patients respond to **PSYCHOANALYSIS** and by positing **THEORIES** (such as **EGO, ID** and **SUPEREGO**) which provide a **STRUCTURE** of thinking.

CONSCIENCE for Freud was a product of experiences in childhood which result in the creation of a **SUPEREGO** – an internal guide which seeks to calm our fears, order our world and resolve conflicts between **EGO** and **ID**. The conscience (superego) is the representative of the voice of our parents who in early childhood produced feelings of pleasure (approval/being loved) and pain (shame/punishment). Various attachments either dissolve (the **OEDIPUS COMPLEX**) or strengthen (gender identification with mother or father), and failure to reconcile a feeling of inner conflict or suppressed desire can lead to depression and **NEUROSIS**.

The structure of Freud's thinking is given on the opposite page, and his theory is sometimes referred to as a **STRUCTURAL THEORY** of the human mind and consciousness. He explains behaviour in terms of the **UNCONSCIOUS** and the sublimation of desire (for example in ideas of God as **FATHER**), or the repression of desire (such as the **LIBIDO** or sexual desire).

Ego

The child develops a sense of **SELF** in relation to the external world. The **EGO** experiences feelings of pleasure and pain and also conscious and unconscious **DESIRES.** The pain of experience propels us towards change but can arise out of **REPRESSION** of urges which become unconscious.

The sense of self begins in childhood with an **IDENTIFICATION** with either **FATHER** or **MOTHER**. The origins of the relationship with the **MOTHER** are explained by the **OEDIPUS COMPLEX** and with the **FATHER** by a process by which the father (**AUTHORITY FIGURE**) becomes part of the infantile stage of the **SUPEREGO**.

CARL JUNG also proposed an **ELECTRA COMPLEX** in 1913 to explain a girl's psychosexual competition with her mother for possession of her father.

The **EGO** thus assumes a regulatory role - it excludes feelings and memories which don't fit our idea of self. For example, this repression resurfaces in **DREAMS** and also **PHOBIAS** – a fear of spiders, for example, which reflect unconscious sources of anxiety. Freud believed the **EGO** was striving to be moral.

The role of **PSYCHOANALYSIS** is to seek to integrate the "coherent ego and the repressed self which is split off from it" (Freud).

Our behaviour (**ACTION**) is a product of both conscious choices and **UNCONSCIOUS** forces 'which exert a driving force without the **EGO** noticing the compulsion" (Freud). These forces result in behaviour which are driven by a complex **PSYCHIC ENERGY** which can leave the human being baffled and confused by their own behaviour – resulting in a feeling of **ANXIETY** or **GUILT**, and **DEPRESSION** (which Freud called 'melancholia').

Id

The **ID** is the seat of feelings, and passions. It is totally non-moral. The origin of the **ID** lies in our **EVOLUTIONARY** background but also in society itself which has conditioned us over generations.

The **ID** develops two broad categories of desire, according to Freud. **EROS** is the life-instinct, which gives us the desires for food, self-preservation, and sex. **THANATOS** is the death-instinct, which drives desires for domination, aggression, violence and self-destruction. These two instincts are at war within the id, and need to be tempered by ego constraints and by **CONSCIENCE**.

Children learn that authorities in the world restrict the extent to which these desires are satisfied. Consequently, humans create the **EGO** which takes account of the realities of the world and society. The ego Freud referred to as the **REALITY PRINCIPLE**, because our awareness of self and of others is crucial to our interaction with the world around us, and is formed at the age of 3 to 5 years.

Within the **ID** there is a battle going on between **EROS** – the life instinct – and **THANATOS** – the death instinct. **EROS** is the 'mischief-maker' (Freud) – the source of uncontrolled passion and also creativity. It is dominated by the **PLEASURE PRINCIPLE**, and yet not all pleasures are felt as acceptable or 'good'. Hence the irrational guilt that can occur over, for example, masturbation and its presence as a **TABOO** in Christianity. Indeed, **EROS** is often at odds with the demands and **CATEGORICAL IMPERATIVES** (Freud's phrase echoing Kant) of the **SUPEREGO**.

The death-instinct (**THANATOS**) is experienced in the desire to kill the **FATHER** and replace him in the mother's affections in the **OEDIPUS COMPLEX**, but is also present in the destructive desires of the **DEPRESSIVE** or self-harming **NEUROTIC**. The death instinct also emerges in **AGGRESSION**, violence and war. In the individual it can have its final expression in **SUICIDE**. But is the positing of a sexual complex just pseudo-science?

Superego

The **SUPEREGO** represents the **INTERNAL** world of **CONSCIENCE**. *"The superego represents the relationship to our parents"* (Freud) and particularly our **FATHER** as authority figure and source of rules and punishments.

To Freud there is a conflict within the human psyche between **EGO** and **ID** and **EROS** and **THANATOS**. A sense of dread emerges in childhood

134

from a fear of castration, a fear of death and a fear of **SEPARATION** from our parents, particularly a fear of loss of the mother's love. The superego can have a destructive power: causing the **EGO** to feel deserted and unloved, abandoned to an anxious and uncertain world and 'fuelling the death-instinct by making the Ego feel abandoned'. This sense of abandonment and powerlessness resurfaces in **DREAMS** (often of failure or of loss of control).

So the **SUPEREGO** can have both a **POSITIVE** and a **NEGATIVE** role – positive in controlling unbridled and anti-social desires and passions, but also **NEGATIVE** in forming an extreme critical voice "brutally chastising and punishing" with guilt, or shame and ultimately a sense of **SELF-HATRED** which cause self-harm and depression.

We can also experience the **SUPEREGO** as **SAVIOUR** and project our guilt and shame onto a sense of **SIN** and a **FATHER-FIGURE** – whom we call **GOD**, who replaces lost love and provides a **SUBLIMINATION** of our sexual desires. Christianity teaches that we deserve death, but that our place is taken by a substitute, Jesus Christ, who removes the **GUILT** and takes on himself the **PUNISHMENT.** (Isaiah 53 "the punishment that makes us whole is upon him"). The **SUPEREGO** in this way grows into a life and power of its own irrespective of the rational thought and reflection of the individual: it is programmed into us by the reactions of other people.

This 'superego', conscience, restricts humans' aggressive powerful desires (**THANATOS** within the **ID**) which would otherwise **DESTROY** us. So guilt "expresses itself in the need for punishment" (Civilisation and its

135

Discontents 1930:315-6). **ERIC FROMM**, quoting Nietzsche, agrees with Freud's analysis of the destructive nature of the **AUTHORITARIAN** conscience.

> "Freud has convincingly demonstrated the correctness of Nietzsche's thesis that the blockage of freedom turns man's instincts 'backward against man himself'. Enmity, cruelty, the delight in persecution...- the turning of all these instincts against their own possessors: this is the origin of the bad conscience". Eric Fromm, Man For Himself, 1947:113

Our superego can lead us to **INTERNALISE** shame, and to experience conflicts between the **ID** desires and the shame emanating from the superego responses. The more we suppress our true feelings, the more that which drives us comes from what Freud described as the **SUBCONSCIOUS**, which like an iceberg lies hidden in the recesses of our minds.

Guilt

Freud believed that the more rapidly the **OEDIPUS COMPLEX** succumbed to **REPRESSION** of our desire for our mother, the stronger will be the domination of the **SUPEREGO** over the **EGO** in the form of a severe and dictatorial **CONSCIENCE**.

So "the tension between the demands of conscience and the actual performances of the ego is experienced in a sense of guilt" (Freud). But guilt can itself be **REPRESSED** and so **UNCONSCIOUS**. Unconscious guilt expresses itself in **NEUROSIS** and other forms of **MENTAL ILLNESS**.

SYNOPTIC POINT Freud sees the structure of our Psyche much as Plato describes it in the analogy of the Charioteer (reason) who seeks to harmonise the twin horses of virtue and passion. A man on horseback (the **EGO**) tries to hold in check the superior strength of the horse (**ID**). But unlike the horseman, the **EGO** uses forces borrowed from the **SUPEREGO** – such as shame and guilt. But a result of this is that **EGO**-identity increasingly fails to represent **ID**-desire. The unfulfilled **ID** resurfaces in sick behaviour or **UNCONSCIOUS** forces (**COMPULSIONS**).

Oedipus Complex

Oedipus so loved his mother that he killed his father and assumed his father's role. Infants start with **MOTHER-ATTACHMENT** which is reinforced by the **PLEASURE PRNCIPLE** as the mother satisfies the infants need for sustenance, love and erotic feeling. The hostility to the **FATHER** gradually subsides in healthy children who become more fully identified with the **MOTHER** (girls) or the **FATHER** (boys) as puberty approaches.

However, a failure to identify successfully with one or other parent can lead to transfer of love (Freud saw this as the origin of **HOMOSEXUAL LOVE**). The **EGO** deepens its relationship with the **ID** in rituals which may be associated with shame, such as masturbation, and fantasies that produce guilt. So the **LIBIDO** can be redirected or even suppressed altogether in a sublimation which we call **RELIGION**.

Ultimately, to Freud, Religion is an infantile projection of our desires and longings onto an image which is an **ILLUSION**. In the Christian Thought paper we study more of this theory in Freud's work, The Future of an Illusion.

Evaluating Freud

Weaknesses

REDUCTIONIST George Klein (1973) argues Freud reduces the human mind to an object of enquiry by positing unprovable theories of how conscious and unconscious processes interact. In so doing he reduces human behaviour to a dualism of 'appropriate' and 'inappropriate' behaviour. Like the criticism levelled at geneticist **RICHARD DAWKINS** we can see this as a form of scientific reductionism.

OVERSEXUALISED Freud argues that the relationship of child and parent has sexual desire through the development of the **OEDIPUS COMPEX** as a key factor. The success or failure of a child's sexual feelings for one or other parent as key to child development is highly contentious. For example, a boy's father is his mother's lover, but he's also the disciplinarian. So, assuming boys do harbour feelings of fear toward their fathers, is this because they fear castration by a romantic rival or because they're afraid of ordinary punishment?

SAMPLING Freud's sample is primarily Austrian upper-class woman, who manifested hysteria. The sample is too small and gender-biased to be truly scientific and the emphasis on sex reveals the cultural repression of that age. Scholars argue Freud fabricates the claim that "almost all of my women patients told me that they had been seduced by their father". John Kihlstrom comments: "While Freud had an enormous impact on 20th century culture, he has been a dead weight on 20th century psychology. The broad themes that Westen writes about were present in psychology before Freud, or arose more recently, independent of his influence. At best, Freud is a figure of only historical interest for psychologists".

Strengths

REVOLUTIONARY Freud was the first person to analyse and theorise about the human unconscious. His argument that dreams are a key to unlocking the secrets of the subconscious mind, his belief that hypnotherapy could change behaviour and his invention of **TALKING THERAPIES** have fundamentally changed our treatment of mental illness.

SECULAR Freud believed religion was a neurosis based on delusions and projections – for example God is a father-substitute onto whom we project our desire for an authority figure, our fear of death and our sense of abandonment. This to Freud was infantile. Westen (1998:35) argues "the notion of unconscious processes is not psychoanalytic voodoo, and it is not the fantasy of muddle-headed clinicians. It is not only clinically indispensable, but it is good science".

HUMANE Freud treated the whole human personality rather than condemning aspects of it as shameful, evil or unacceptable. He thereby challenged the old religious **DUALISMS** of good versus evil, monster versus hero, to give a humane alternative and offering hope of cure and transformation to those whose lives were blighted by mental health problems.

Key Quotes - Freud

"In the Ego and the Id Freud abandons the simple dichotomy between instinct and consciousness and recognizes the unconscious elements of the ego and superego, the importance of nonsexual impulses (aggression or the 'death instinct'), and the alliance between superego and id, superego and aggression". Christopher Lasch The Culture of Narcissism page 32

"While Freud had an enormous impact on 20th century culture, he has been a dead weight on 20th century psychology. The broad themes were present in psychology before Freud, or arose in more recently independent of his influence. At best, Freud is a figure of only historical interest for psychologists." John Kihlstrom

"When we were little children we knew these higher natures of our parents, and later we took them into ourselves". Freud

"All that is repressed is unconscious, but not all that is unconscious is repressed". Freud

"To the ego, living means the same as being loved". Freud

"By setting up the superego, the ego has mastered the Oedipus Complex and placed itself in subjection to the Id". Freud

"The tension between the demands of conscience and the performance of the ego is experienced as guilt". Freud

"As the child was once under the domination of its parents, so the ego submits to the Categorical Imperative of the superego". Freud

"Human megalomania will have suffered its third and most wounding blow from the psychological research of the present time which seeks to prove to the ego that it is not even master in its own house". Freud

Evaluation - Psychological Approaches

These psychological accounts of conscience undermine **AQUINAS'** religious theory of conscience (see below) because conscience is **ENVIRONMENTALLY INDUCED** by upbringing, not innate.

Freud's theory is highly **DETERMINISTIC**, because humans are driven, according to Freud, by forces operating out of our subconscious minds.

PSYCHOLOGY doesn't rule out the possibility that God has some involvement with conscience (in originating a moral faculty, for example), but if environment operates so strongly on conscience the religious theories need reworking.

A Theology of Conscience

Key Terms

- **CONSCIENTIA** Aquinas' definition of conscience as 'reason making right decisions".

- **SYNDERESIS** Aquinas' definition of conscience as our innate ability and desire to orientate ourselves towards good ends (aim at the **PRIMARY PRECEPTS**).

- **PHRONESIS** Practical wisdom or right judgement.

- **VINCIBLE IGNORANCE** Blameworthy ignorance of something which we should in principle know about eg a 30 mph zone.

- **INVINCIBLE IGNORANCE** Ignorance which we can't be blamed for - eg a Borneo tribesman's ignorance of Jesus Christ.

St **PAUL** argued that all human beings, Jew and Gentile (non-Jew), possessed an **INNATE** knowledge of God's law, (we're born with it) written on our hearts. *"I do not do the thing I want, the very thing I hate is what I do"* he wrote in **ROMANS 7** and Gentiles have God's law *"engraved on their hearts"*, (Romans 2:15).

John Henry **NEWMAN** (1801-1890) was an Anglican priest who converted to Rome. How could a good Catholic accept papal **INFALLIBILITY** and still follow his conscience? Newman describes conscience as the innate **VOICE OF GOD** and **ABORIGINAL** (= original or native) **VICAR OF CHRIST**.

> "It is a principle planted in us before we have had any training" argued Newman. Newman quoted the fourth Lateran Council when he said "he who acts against conscience loses his soul". John Henry Newman

AQUINAS (1224-1274) agrees with St Paul and with Newman, as he distinguished between an innate source of good and evil, **SYNDERESIS** (literally, one who watches over us) and a judgement derived from our reason, **CONSCIENTIA**. This second idea is, however, closer to **JOSEPH BUTLER**.

Synderesis and Conscience

Thomas Aquinas saw **SYNDERESIS** (first of two words for conscience) as an innate instinct for distinguishing right from wrong that orientates **DESIRE** and forms the **WILL**. Synderesis can be defined as:

> "A natural disposition of the human mind by which we instinctively understand the first principles of morality". Aquinas

Aquinas (optimistically) thought people tended towards goodness and away from evil (the **SYNDERESIS** principle). This principle is the starting point or **FIRST PRINCIPLE** of Aquinas' **NATURAL LAW** system of ethics. So these 'first principles' are the **PRIMARY PRECEPTS** which we observe rational human beings pursue as goals. These include preservation of life, ordered society, worship of God, education and reproduction (acronym **POWER**).

Structure of Thought

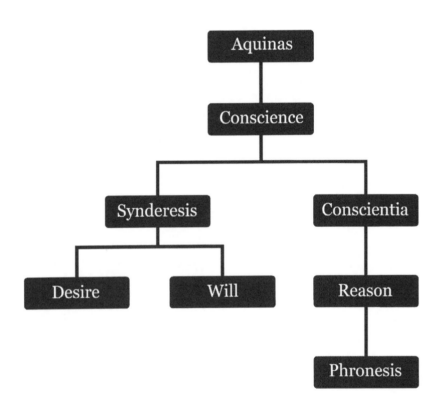

CONSCIENTIA is the power of reason for working out what is good and what is evil, the *"application of knowledge to activity"* (Aquinas). This is something closer to moral judgement rather than instinct, close to Aristotle's **PHRONESIS** or practical wisdom or **BUTLER**'s determining processs for distinguishing between **SELF-INTEREST** and **BENEVOLENCE**. We cannot flourish without it. In practical situations we have to make choices and to weigh alternatives, and we do so by using our conscience. One way we do this is by looking at consequences and applying the **PRINCIPLE OF DOUBLE EFFECT** (when we have to kill a foetus to save a mother's life we have a good intention but a double effect of one good and one evil consequence).

Conscience can make mistakes and needs to be trained in wisdom. At times people do bad things because they make a mistake in discriminating good from evil. Aquinas believed that if the conscience has made a **FACTUAL** mistake, for example, if I don't realise that my action breaks a particular rule, then my mistaken conscience is not to blame.

But if I am simply **IGNORANT** of the rule (such as not committing adultery), I am to blame. Taking a rather bizarre example, Aquinas argues that if a man sleeps with another man's wife thinking she was his wife, then he is not morally blameworthy because he acted "in good faith".

"Conscience is reason making right decisions and not a voice giving us commands". Aquinas

Conscience deliberates between good and bad. Aquinas notes two dimensions of moral decision making, "Man's reasoning is a kind of movement which begins with the understanding of certain things that are naturally known as **IMMUTABLE** principles without investigation. It ends in the intellectual activity by which we make judgements on the basis of those principles". Aquinas

So **SYNDERESIS** is right **INSTINCT** or habit, the natural tendency humans have to do good and avoid evil. **CONSCIENTIA** is right **REASON**, which distinguishes between right and wrong as we make practical moral decisions. We see how conscientia works itself out in the **PRINCIPLE OF DOUBLE EFFECT,** when we solve a genuine moral dilemma, when two 'good things' conflict and we can't have both.

Vincible and Invincible Ignorance

INVINCIBLE IGNORANCE occurs when people (such as non-Christians or tribes in Borneo) are ignorant of the moral law not because they refuse to believe, but rather because they've not yet had an opportunity to hear and experience it. St. Thomas Aquinas discusses the topic in his Summa Theologica 1-1 Q97. Pope Pius IX used the term in his 1854 document Singulari Quadam .

In his 1963 sermon, "Strength to Love," Martin Luther King wrote, *"Nothing in all the world is more dangerous than sincere ignorance and conscientious stupidity."* Intentional **VINCIBLE** ignorance is when I deliberately act on ignorance. For example, if I choose to fire my rifle into a forest without first making sure there's no-one in the undergrowth picking blackberries, I am "vincibly" ignorant and morally culpable for my actions if I wound someone.

Joseph Butler - Innate Conscience Guided by Reason

Butler (1692-1752), former Bishop of Durham, believed human beings had two natural rational guides to behaviour: enlightened self-interest and conscience. Greeks like **EPICURUS** would have recognised the self-interest of the pursuit of **HAPPINESS**, but not the idea of an **INNATE** (inborn) disposition of conscience.

Butler believed we were naturally moral, and that conscience was the **SUPREME AUTHORITY** in moral actions. Morality was part of our human natures.

Human nature has a **HIERARCHY OF VALUES** with conscience at the top which than adjudicates between the self-love and **BENEVOLENCE** (= doing good to others) which define us as human beings. Conscience helps the selfish human become virtuous and so provides a **BALANCE** between these two tendencies.

Butler doesn't deny we have feelings and passions, but it is conscience which **JUDGES** between them as the "moral approving and disapproving faculty" and we act **PROPORTIONATELY** (appropriately to the situation) according to our conscience.

The guidance is **INTUITIVE**, given by God but still the voice of **REASON**. He is arguing that each human being has direct insight into the **UNIVERSAL** or objective rightness or wrongness of an action.

Evaluation - Butler

Butler attacked the **EGOISM** of Thomas Hobbes. **BENEVOLENCE** is as much part of our shared human nature as **SELF-LOVE**. Here there are echoes of Richard **DAWKINS**' argument that we all share a biologically evolved "altruistic gene" (altruism = concern for others).

Butler sees an **OBJECTIVE MORAL ORDER** in the world. Fortune and misfortune are not entirely arbitrary – if we choose **VICE** we naturally suffer misfortune. Following the dictates of conscience usually leads to **HAPPINESS**. But in the end it's **GOD** who guarantees the consequences turn out best. "Although Butler's description of conscience is **UNSURPASSED**, he gives no definition of conscience". D.D.Raphael

> "Common behaviour all over the world is formed on a supposition of a moral faculty; whether called conscience, moral reason, moral sense, or divine reason; whether considered as a sentiment of understanding, or as a perception of the heart". Joseph Butler

Authoritarian Conscience - Eric Fromm

Eric **FROMM** experienced all the evil of Nazism and wrote his books to reflect on how conscience and freedom can be subverted even in the most civilised societies. In order to explain how, for example, Adolf **EICHMANN** can plead at his trial for mass murder in 1961 that he was only "following orders" in applying the final solution, we can invoke Fromm's idea of the authoritarian conscience.

The authoritarian conscience is the **INTERNALISED VOICE** of the external authority, something close to Freud's concept of the superego considered above. It's backed up by fear of punishment, or spurred on by admiration or can even be created because I idolise an authority figure, as Unity **MITFORD** did Adolf Hitler.

As Unity found, this blinds us to the faults of the idolised figure, and causes us to become **SUBJECT** to that person's will, so that "the laws and sanctions of the externalised authority become part of oneself" (1947:108).

So, as with the Nazis, ordinary seemingly civilised human beings do **ATROCIOUS EVIL** because they are subject to a voice which comes essentially from outside them, bypassing their own moral sense. This authoritarian conscience can come from:

PROJECTION onto someone of an image of perfection.

The experience of parental **RULES** or expectations.

An adopted **BELIEF** system, such as a religion, with its own authority structure.

"Good conscience is consciousness of pleasing authority, guilty conscience is consciousness of displeasing it". Eric Fromm (1947:109)

The individual's **IDENTITY** and sense of security has become wrapped up in the authority figure, and the voice inside is really someone else's voice. This also means **OBEDIENCE** becomes the cardinal virtue, and as the Nazi Adolf Eichmann pleaded at his trial. **AUTONOMY** and **CREATIVITY** are lost.

"Those subject to him are means to his end and, consequently his property, and used by him for his purposes." Fromm (1947:112)

DESTRUCTIVE TENDENCIES emerge, Fromm stresses, where "a person takes on the role of authority by treating himself with the same cruelty and strictness" and "destructive energies are discharged by taking on the role of the authority and dominating oneself as servant". (1947:113)

"Paradoxically, authoritarian guilty conscience is a result of feelings of strength, independence, productiveness and pride, while the authoritarian good conscience springs from feelings of obedience, dependence, powerlessness and sinfulness". Fromm (1947:112)

The Humanistic Conscience

The **HUMANISTIC** conscience, Fromm suggests is "our own voice, present in every human being, and independent of external sanctions and rewards" (1947:118). Fromm sees this voice as our **TRUE SELVES**, found by listening to ourselves and heeding our deepest needs, desires and goals.

> *"Different from the authoritarian conscience is the "humanistic conscience"; this is the voice present in every human being and independent from external sanctions and rewards. Humanistic conscience is based on the fact that as human beings we have an intuitive knowledge of what is human and inhuman, what is conducive of life and what is destructive of life. This conscience serves our functioning as human beings. It is the voice which calls us back to ourselves, to our humanity".* Eric Fromm

The result of so listening is to release **HUMAN POTENTIAL** and creativity, and to become what we potentially are; "the goal is productiveness, and therefore, happiness" (1947:120). This is something gained over a life of learning, reflection and setting and realising goals for ourselves.

Fromm sees **KAFKA**'s "The Trial" as a parable of how the two consciences in practice live together. A man is arrested, he knows not on what charge or pretext. He seems powerless to prevent a terrible fate - his own death - at the hands of this alien authority. But just before he dies he gains a glimpse of another person (Fromm's more developed **HUMANISTIC CONSCIENCE**) looking at him from an upstairs room.

Key Confusions

1. "Conscience is a form of consciousness". No, conscience is only a form of consciousness if it is clearly an exercise of choice and reason, as in Aquinas' **CONSCIENTIA** or Butler's principle of judgement between self-interest and benevolence. But Freud argues **UNCONSCIOUS** forces drive guilt feelings which drive conscience - and these forces may be irrational or **NEUROTIC**.

2. "Without God there can be no human conscience". Only in a certain (narrow) Christian world view that sees even our moral sense corrupted by sin. To Aquinas we all share in **SYNDERESIS** which means conscience is a **UNIVERSAL** phenomenon we possess by virtue of our creation in the **IMAGE OF GOD.** It doesn't matter if we believe in God or not.

3. "Science cannot explain conscience". Richard **DAWKINS** would disagree. The **SELFISH GENE** is actually the **SELF-PRESERVING** gene and evolution has given us a genetic predisposition to **ALTRUISM.** So when the conscience of a distinguished Leeds surgeon caused him to jump into the surf off Cornwall to try to save two teenaged swimmers in distress in 2015, he was showing the **ALTRUISTIC** (help others) gene. He tragically died in this heroic moral action.

Possible Future Exam Questions

1. Critically evaluate the theories of conscience of Aquinas and Freud.

2. "Conscience is given by God, not formed by childhood experience". Critically evaluate this view with reference to Freud and Aquinas.

3. "Conscience is a product of culture, environment, genetic predisposition and education". Discuss

4. "Conscience is another word for irrational feelings of guilt". Discuss

5. "Freud's theory of conscience has no scientific basis. It is merely hypothesis". Discuss

6. 'Guilt feelings are induced by social relationships as a method of control". Discuss

Key Quotes - Conscience

"Freud has convincingly demonstrated the correctness of Nietzsche's thesis that the blockage of freedom turns man's instincts 'backward against man himself'. Enmity, cruelty, the delight in persecution - the turning of all these instincts against their own possessors: this is the origin of the bad conscience". Eric Fromm

"Conscience does not only offer itself to show us the way we should walk in, but it likewise carries its own authority with it, that it is our natural guide,

the guide assigned us by the Author of our nature; it therefore belongs to our condition of being, it is our duty to walk in its path". Joseph Butler

"Conscience is reason making right decisions and not a voice giving us commands". Aquinas

"The Gentiles can demonstrate the effects of the law engraved on their hearts, to which their own conscience bears witness". Rom 2.15

"Conscience is the built in monitor of moral action or choice values". John Macquarrie

Suggested Reading

Aquinas Summa Theologica 1-1 Q79 (see peped.org/conscience/extracts)

Freud, S. The Ego and the Id Createspace Independent Publishing Platform (22 Mar. 2010)

Fromm, E. (1947) Man for Himself: An Inquiry into the Psychology of Ethics London: Routledge, IV.2

Internet Encyclopaedia of Philosophy, Sigmund Freud, http://www.iep.utm.edu/freud/ (See peped.org/conscience/extracts)

Kihlstrom, John F. (2015). Personality (Pearson) and The Psychological Unconscious. In L.R. Pervin & O. John (Eds.), Handbook of personality, 2nd ed. (pp. 424-442). New York: Guilford. http://socrates.berkeley.edu/~kihlstrm/PersonalityWeb/Ch8CritiquePsychoanalysis.htm

Macmillan, M.B. (1996).Freud evaluated: The completed arc. Cambridge, Ma.: MIT Press.

Strohm, P. (2011) Conscience: A Very Short Introduction, Oxford University Press, Chapters 1 and 3

Westen, D. (1998). The Scientific Legacy of Sigmund Freud. Psychological Bulletin,124, 333-371

Sexual Ethics

Issues Surrounding Sexual Ethics

What does it mean to be **HUMAN**? Is there one **UNIVERSAL** shared human nature (as **NATURAL LAW** suggests)?

Are gender equality and same sex attraction equally ethical issues? Or do we evaluate them as good or bad in the light of **CONSEQUENCES** and **HAPPINESS** produced by social policy and individual action, as the **UTILITARIANS** suggest?

What values give meaning to sexual relationships (such as fidelity, chastity and commitment – which seem to be changing)? Are the **VIRTUES** of human character a better way of analysing this issue?

How have developments in understanding the biology and **PSYCHOLOGY** of the human person affected sexual ethics? Sexual ethics thus shares concerns and insights from **PSYCHOLOGY**, **BIOLOGY**, and **SOCIOLOGY**. With the prevalence of pornography, sex trafficking and decline in old models of family life, there can be few more pressing ethical issues facing us. The specification identifies three issues:

- **PRE-MARITAL SEX**

- **EXTRA-MARITAL SEX (ADULTERY)**

- **HOMOSEXUALITY**

Structure of Thought

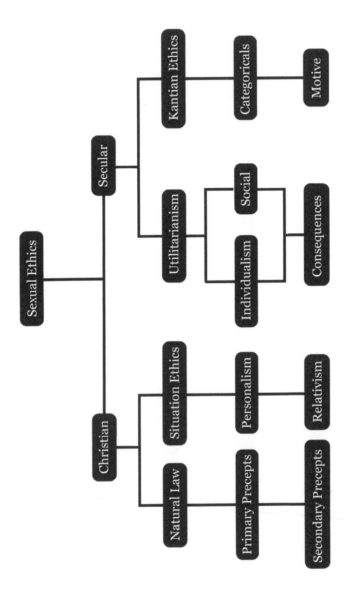

Sex & Evolution

Homo Sapiens emerged around 150,000 years ago. As social life developed so a primitive **MORALITY** created rules and boundaries around sexual intercourse. Sex changes its function from **REPRODUCTION** to **SOCIAL REGULATION**.

Religions emerge that created **PURITY CODES**. These involved **TABOOS** (the declaration of certain practices as unclean). For example the purity code of the Hebrew Bible, **LEVITICUS**, lays down a code of uncleanness – which included **BLOOD, INCEST, ADULTERY**, and **SAME SEX RELATIONS**. These are abominations punishable by social exclusion or death.

Such attitudes are reflected in attitudes to **WOMEN**. Women came to be seen as **PROPERTY** of men. Virginity was prized. Up to 1872, married women in Britain had to surrender all property to their husbands; there was no concept of marital rape until 1991 and violence against married women was only outlawed in 1861. In 2011 there were 443 reported incidents of "honour crime" (violence, forced marriage and even murder) in the UK.

A concept of what is **NATURAL** emerged and with it psychological **GUILT** for those who did not conform. It's hard to believe that in 1899 **OSCAR WILDE** was jailed for two years hard labour for a homosexual relationship. **HOMOSEXUAL SEX** was only legalised in 1967. The last people to be executed for sodomy in England were James Pratt (1805–1835) and John Smith (1795–1835), in November 1835.

Kinsey & the Sexual Revolution

The **KINSEY REPORT** of 1945 shocked America.   Intimate surveys of real people's preferences revealed:

- 10% of men were homosexual for at least three years of their lives. How then could sexual preference be **UNCHANGING**, fixed and uniform?

- 26% of married women had extramarital experiences of different sorts.

- 90% of men masturbated.

- 50% of men had been unfaithful to their wives.

Christian Views on Sex

NATURAL LAW

Aquinas taught that there were three rational ends of sex, arising from the **PRIMARY PRECEPT** of reproduction:

- To have children.

- To give **PLEASURE**.

- To bind husband and wife together.

His view – that sex was for pleasure, was widely condemned, Aquinas wrote "the exceeding pleasure experienced in sex does not destroy the balance of nature as long as it is in harmony with reason". Right reason involves a delicate balance of the three purposes of sex – and avoidance of irrational or animal extremes. So the following sexual sins were forbidden:

- **RAPE**

- **CASUAL SEX**

- **ADULTERY**

- **HOMOSEXUAL SEX**

- **MASTURBATION**

Aquinas' view echoed the erotic celebration of sexual ecstasy in the **SONG OF SONGS** in the Hebrew Bible where sex is a sacred gift and picture of a mystical union, and one of the highest spiritual as well as physical forms of being.

Behold you are beautiful, my love;

behold you are beautiful;

your eyes are like doves,

Behold you are beautiful my beloved, truly lovely....

Your two breasts are like two fawns,

161

twins of a gazelle that feed among the lilies...

You have ravished my heart with a glance of your eyes .

(Song of Songs 1:15; 4:2, 5 & 9)

This is one of two parallel strains in the Bible – one positive and one negative, and the positive strain, that sex is to be **CELEBRATED** is echoed by Jesus himself, quoting Genesis 2:24, "from the beginning God created them male and female, and for this reason a man shall leave his mother and father and be united with his wife, and the two shall become one flesh. So what God has joined together, let no-one divide" (Mark 10:6-9). See also Paul in Ephesians 5:31.

THE NEGATIVE STRAIN - THEOLOGY OF THE FALL

There is also a negative strain in Christianity which sees sex as dangerous, unclean, and sexual pleasure as sinful.

AUGUSTINE wrote that marriage was the *"first fellowship of humankind in this mortal life"*, and *"good not just for producing children, but also because of the natural friendship between the sexes"*, although primarily *"a remedy for weakness, and source of comfort"*. Ultimately the good of marriage lay in its *"goodness, fidelity and unbreakable bond"*.

Augustine argued against the **PELAGIANS** who saw sexual pleasure as a **NATURAL GOOD**, evil only in excess. Augustine agreed with Paul that since the **FALL** the body had been subject to death, *"our body weighs heavy on our soul"* with its sinful desires. Augustine believed that since the fall desire had been tainted by **LUST**. So sexual pleasure in marriage needed to be moderated by reason.

Sexual desire ("the carnal appetite") outside marriage, and sexual activity that results, *"is not good , but an evil that comes from original sin"*. This evil of carnal lust can invade even marriage – so it is **DANGEROUS** and needs to be treated wisely and carefully.

After the **FALL** (Genesis 3) men and women were *"naked and ashamed"*. The man's member is *"no longer obedient to a quiet and normal will"*. Humankind was in danger of running away with lust for each other.

CONCLUSION: Augustine argues that precisely because the body is created good, it can be used wrongly, and this goodness has been deeply stained by the Fall. Sexual desire has to be circumscribed by **MODESTY**, chastity and wisdom.

CATHOLIC TEACHING TODAY

The Roman Catholic Church teaches that sex has two functions – procreative and **UNITIVE** (binding two people together). Procreation is primary. According to Humanae Vitae (1967) these two elements are **INSEPARABLE**.

> *"Sexuality becomes fully human when it is integrated into the relationship of one person to the other in lifelong gift of a man to a woman".* Catechism 2338

CHASTITY is the virtue of self-mastery (Catechism 2339). It is expressed in friendship towards our neighbour. Sex outside marriage is *"gravely contrary to the dignity of persons and of human sexuality which is naturally ordered to the procreation of children".* Catechism 2354

HOMOSEXUAL ACTS are "intrinsically disordered". *"They are contrary to the natural law. They close the sexual act to the gift of life. Under no circumstances can they be approved".* Catechism 2358

ADULTERY is absolutely forbidden by the sixth commandment and Jesus' words.

CONTRACEPTION - in 1951 Pope Pius XII officially permitted the rhythm method, but otherwise **HUMANAE VITAE** (1967) upholds the view that anything that breaks the natural relationship between sex and conception is wrong.

Evaluation - Catholic View

Professor Peter **GOMES** of Harvard University argues that the Bible bans one **CULTURAL** expression of homosexuality – a promiscuous one and *"never contemplated a form of homosexuality in which loving and faithful persons sought to live out the implications of the gospel with as much fidelity as any heterosexual believer".* The Good Book (1997)

The Catholic interpretation of **NATURAL LAW** implies that the primary function of sex is reproduction. But suppose the primary purpose is **BONDING**, then the argument that sex is purely for reproduction falls down — we can be Natural Law theorists and disagree about the secondary precepts (which Aquinas always argues are relative).

The Catholic **ASSUMPTION** (following Aquinas) is of one human nature. But psychology suggests there are varieties of human nature (heterosexual, homosexual, bisexual) because of genes or environment.

The prohibition on **CONTRACEPTION** seems irrational in a world of overpopulation and **STD**s. If **PRESERVATION OF LIFE** conflicts with **REPRODUCTION**, surely preservation of life is the primary **PRIMARY PRECEPT**?

Situation Ethics - Christian Relativism

Joseph **FLETCHER** sees his own theory as **RELATIVISTIC** (even though it retains one absolute principle, agape love) because any decision is made relative to circumstances.

ABSOLUTE rules must be rejected as authoritarian and unloving.

Biblical prescriptions should be followed as wise **ADVICE** but abandoned in extreme situations if love demands it.

Fletcher argues that many applications of morality are never discussed in the Bible: "Jesus said nothing about birth control, homosexuality, pre-marital intercourse , homosexuality, sex play, petting or courtship". (Fletcher, page 80).

"It seems impossible to see any sound reason for any of the attempts to legislate morality. It is doubtful whether love's cause is helped by any of the sex laws that try to dictate sexual practices for consenting adults". (Fletcher, Situation Ethics, page 80)

AGAPE love (unconditional love) is the only norm. The situationist is not a 'what asker', ("what sexual practice is allowed?) but a 'who asker'. It's about **PERSONALISM** – people come first.

Evaluation - Situation Ethics (Christian Relativism)

AGAPE is too high a standard for our personal relationships, usually governed by self-interest. Why should I be loving (rather than pleasure-seeking)?

The vulnerable (young, homeless, poor) need the protection of laws preventing **ABUSE** and **EXPLOITATION**.

We cannot predict **CONSEQUENCES** eg unwanted pregnancies or **STD**s happen to people not expecting them who may honestly believe they love the other person.

Homosexual Acts - a Test Case

We have already seen that the Catholic Church condemns homosexual behaviour as intrinsically disordered because of the assumption of one

UNIFORM HUMAN NATURE. The situationist takes the opposite view; such legalism is unloving and so wrong. Is there a middle way?

In the **ANGLICAN** church there are two gay bishops (in America) and many practising gay priests. **VIRTUE ETHICS** indicates there is a third way of analysing homosexual behaviour. Which **VIRTUES** are present in the relationship? The **EXCESS** of promiscuity is condemned, but faithfulness, care and compassion can apply in any relationship irrespective of orientation. By the same argument the **DEFICIENCY** of abstinence is also a character **VICE**.

The moral issue surrounding homosexuality should therefore be about the promiscuous lifestyle and irresponsible spread of disease (as with heterosexuals). The legalism of natural law or over-emphasis on the code of Leviticus blinds us to the true moral question. What **VALUES** do we need in order to **FLOURISH**?

Kant on Sex

Kant asks us to commit to build the moral world – the **SUMMUM BONUM** or greatest good, by following the rational principle he calls the **CATEGORICAL IMPERATIVE**. This principle has to be applied in all similar circumstances without conditions – it is **ABSOLUTE**. We have to act in such a way that we can imagine a universal law where everyone follows the rule that is generated.

Humans have intrinsic **VALUE** as "ends in themselves". We must be given equal dignity and respect as autonomous rational beings.

We share an irrational nature of passions and instincts with **ANIMALS** but we can rise above these and order our lives by reason. Human sex will be different from animal urges.

LUST disturbs reason. By desiring someone simply as an object of pleasure (rather than seeing them as a whole person, with dignity and reason) we dishonour them and violate their special uniqueness as a free person. We sink to the level of animals.

> "Sex exposes mankind to the danger of equality with the beasts...by virtue of the nature of sexual desire a person who sexually desires another person objectifies that person..and makes of the loved person an object of appetite. As soon as that appetite is satisfied one casts aside the person as one casts aside a lemon that has been sucked dry".
> Kant, Lectures on Ethics

MARRIAGE is the best expression of our sexuality. The pleasure of sex is acceptable (ie not animal) because two people surrender their dignity to each other and permit each other's bodies to be used for this purpose – it is a mutual **CONSENSUAL CONTRACT**. Reproduction is not the end of sex, Kant argues, but lifelong surrender to each other in a context of love and respect.

Evaluation of Kant

Kant appears to separate our **ANIMAL** nature from our **RATIONAL**. This dualism explains why he still sees sex as something belonging to the animal nature. But **FEELINGS** and **REASON** cannot be separated this way, many would argue.

Kantian ethics produces **ABSOLUTES** (Categoricals). So the absolute "no sex before marriage" applies here. But in the modern era such absolutes seem to deny the possibility of a **TEMPORARY** committed relationship – or even sex for fun.

It's possible to be a Kantian and accept **HOMOSEXUAL MARRIAGE** but not **ADULTERY**.

Utilitarianism - Balancing the Positive and the Negative

What do the utilitarians say about our four issues: contraception, pre-marital sex, adultery and homosexuality? Here we contrast two utilitarians: **MILL** (1806-73) and **SINGER** (1946-).

Mill is a **MULTILEVEL** utilitarian who follows a more **ARISTOTELEAN** idea of happiness – **EUDAIMONIA** or personal and social flourishing. He argues that we need **RULES** to protect justice and **RIGHTS**, which are the cumulative wisdom of society. But when happiness demands it, or a **CONFLICT** of values occurs, we revert to being an **ACT** utilitarian — hence multilevel (Act and Rule) utilitarianism.

Mill agreed that **CONTRACEPTION** was moral as it increased personal and social happiness, through family planning and restrictions on population growth. Today the British Humanist association writes "if contraception results in every child being a wanted child and in better, healthier lives for women, it must be a good thing". Mill was imprisoned in 1832 for distributing "diabolical handbills" advocating contraception.

Mill had found a murdered baby in a park. The practice of exposing unwanted children was widespread. Hospitals for **FOUNDLINGS** such as **CORAM** set up in Bristol in 1741, did little except institutionalise **INFANTICIDE** (child killing). Between 1728 and 1757 33% of babies born in foundling hospitals and workhouses died or were killed.

On **HOMOSEXUAL** rights Mill follows Bentham in arguing for "utilitarian equality" by which everyone's happiness counts equally. Bentham was the first philosopher to suggest legalised **SODOMY** in an unpublished paper in 1802. Freedom was a key to personal flourishing, and as long as no harm was done to any but consenting adults, (Mill's **HARM PRINCIPLE** in On Liberty) it is a private matter how people order their sex lives.

In his essay on **LIBERTY** (1859) Mill argues for **SOCIAL RIGHTS** so we can undertake "experiments in living" that give us protection from the prejudices of popular culture and "the tyranny of prevailing opinion and feeling". Mill would have approved of **COHABITATION** and pre-marital sex.

Evaluation - Mill

Mill was a father of the **LIBERALISM** we take for granted where difference is tolerated. His brand of utilitarianism balances social **JUSTICE** and individual freedom and pursuit of happiness.

Utilitarianism works well looking **BACKWARDS**. The Abortion Act (1967), the Homosexual Reform Act (1967) and the Divorce Reform Act (1969) are all examples of utilitarian legislation.

Utilitarian ethics works less well looking forwards. We cannot predict **CONSEQUENCES**. So the **AIDS** epidemic can be seen as a product partly of personal freedom to adopt a promiscuous "unsafe" lifestyle. It is hard to see how a utilitarian can prevent this or even argue it is wrong if freely chosen.

Many of the greatest **SOCIAL** reforms have not been inspired by Christian values, Natural Law or Kantian ethics, but by **UTILITARIAN** considerations of social **WELFARE**. Today relatively few Christian churches accept the complete equality of women.

Preference Utilitarianism

Peter Singer defends the utilitarian line advanced by Mill and argued that, with **HOMOSEXUALITY**, *"If a form of sexual activity brings satisfaction to those who take part in it, and harms no-one, what can be immoral about it?"*

On **ADULTERY** preference utilitarians approve of any sexual activity which maximises the preferences of individuals, taking account the preferences of all those affected. So incest, bestiality, or adultery would all be acceptable.

Singer as argues for **CONTRACEPTION** as population growth is one of the most pressing utilitarian issues, we should "help governments make contraception and sterilisation as widespread as possible" (Practical Ethics, page 183). But overseas aid should be made conditional on adoption of contraceptives.

Key Confusions

- "Sexual ethics is merely up to individual choice". It is a common misunderstanding of ethics that it is purely about personal choice. Yet **MILL** points out, following **ARISTOTLE**, that ethics always has a personal and a social dimension. Laws both reflect social morality and also help to mould it. So when the law was changed on homosexuality, contraception and child protection it both reflected a change in social attitudes (things once thought acceptable are now seen to be abusive and other things once criminalised are now morally accepted) and helped to form those attitudes. And if I choose to be promiscuous that affects every person I am promiscuous with.

- "Sexual behaviour is natural and doesn't do anyone any harm". This is a misunderstanding of what 'natural' means in ethics. For example, the word 'natural" in **NATURAL LAW** means 'in line with our rational natural purpose'. Certain goals are unique to human beings - for example **WORSHIP OF GOD** and even those shared with animals (**REPRODUCTION**) function in a different way to animals - we are **MORAL** beings capable of evaluating consequences, for example, and capable of understanding our social responsibility to build an orderly and co-operative society.

- "There is one heterosexual human nature". This is an **ASSUMPTION** of natural law theory which appears highly questionable. It seems there really is a **HOMOSEXUAL** human nature and also a **TRANSGENDER** human nature. The whole ethics of sexual behaviour has altered radically in the light of empirical research (such as the **KINSEY** report) and also the insights of psychologists such as **FREUD** and **JUNG**. Moreover the criticisms of a type of religious thought that equates sex with **SIN** may well still hang over in the **GUILT** that attends certain expressions of sexual behaviour. Of course, which expression is part of our ongoing ethical debate.

Possible Future Exam Questions

1. "Religion is irrelevant in deciding issues surrounding sexual behaviour". Discuss

2. Critically evaluate the view that the ethics of sexual behaviour should be entirely private and personal.

3. "Because sexual conduct affects others, it should be subject to legislation". Discuss

4. "Normative theories are useful in what they might say about sexual ethics". Discuss

Key Quotes - Sexual Ethics

"The only purpose for which power can be rightfully exercised over any member of a civilised community against his will, is to prevent harm to others. His own good, either physical or moral, is not sufficient warrant". JS Mill

"If a form of sexual activity brings satisfaction to those who take part in it, and harms no-one, what can be immoral about it?" Peter Singer

"The pleasure derived from the union between the sexes is a pleasure: therefore, leaving aside the evils, which derive from that source here is why the legislator must do whatever is in his power so that the quantity in society is as high as possible". Jeremy Bentham

"Sex exposes mankind to the danger of equality with the beasts...by virtue of the nature of sexual desire a person who sexually desires another person objectifies that person..and makes of the loved person an object of appetite. As soon as that appetite is satisfied one casts aside the person as one casts aside a lemon that has been sucked dry ". Kant

"It seems impossible to see any sound reason for any of the attempts to legislate morality. It is doubtful whether love's cause is helped by any of the sex laws that try to dictate sexual practices for consenting adults". Joseph Fletcher

Suggested Reading

Aquinas On Marriage Summa Theologica II-II Q153 a. 2c, a. 3c, q. 154 a. Extract available on Peped's sexualethicsteachingresources.co.uk website)

Pope Paul VI (1968) Humanae Vitae (Available on Peped's sexualethicsteachingresources.co.uk website)

Church of England House of Bishops (1991) Issues in Human Sexuality, London: Church House Publishing

Mill, J.S. (1859) On Liberty, Chapter 1

The Four Questions Answered

In the first section of this book I mentioned that there are four questions we need to ask of any moral theory. They spell the acronym **DARM** (**D**erivation, **A**pplication, **R**ealism, **M**otivation).

1. HOW IS THE IDEA OF GOODNESS DERIVED?

Goodness has to come from somewhere – it is, after all a human construct. The normal candidates are three:

1. God or faith

2. Reason (a priori)

3. Observation or experience (a posteriori, from experience).

RELATIVISTS argue that our idea of goodness comes directly from **CULTURE** (what JL Mackie in Inventing Right and Wrong calls "forms of life") or from **EXPERIENCE** (the utilitarian or situationist view that we judge right and wrong according to circumstances and likely consequences).

NATURAL LAW theorists like **AQUINAS** argue that goodness is partly an **A PRIORI** idea given by God – what he calls synderesis "the intuitive knowledge of first principles", and partly an **A POSTERIORI** idea worked out by experience. We develop our conscience and practical wisdom by looking at circumstances . Natural Law goods are in the end

OBSERVABLE GOODS. We apply the **PRIMARY PRECEPTS** (acronym **POWER**) to situations.

KANT argues that morality is an **A PRIORI** category of the mind like number or cause and effect. Just as we need a concept of **NUMBER** before we can count, so we need a concept of the **CATEGORICAL IMPERATIVE** before we can apply it to the world and synthetic experience where we discover how it works. Morality is therefore **A PRIORI SYNTHETIC**.

UTLITARIANS see goodness as a **TELEOLOGICAL** idea depending on the end we pursue, either **PLEASURE** (the psychological "sovereign two masters, pleasure and pain" of Bentham) or **HAPPINESS** (it is good because most people desire it as an end in itself, says **MILL**). So goodness is measurable, an **OBJECTIVE, EMPIRICAL IDEA**, either by counting **HEDONS** (Bentham) or **DESIRES** (Mill). This is therefore a theory appealing to **A POSTERIORI** knowledge because we cannot know consequences without some experience of them.

Notice that only one theory is purely **DEONTOLOGICAL**, Kantian ethics. **NATURAL LAW** has deontological outcomes (the **SECONDARY PRECEPTS**) which come from a **TELEOLOGICAL WORLDVIEW** because in Natural law everything has a proper rational purpose (**TELOS**).

SITUATION ETHICS argues that goodness is accepted by faith as the supreme noram (**POSITIVISM**). Fletcher makes it clear that no intrinsic good can be proved (be it the good will, happiness or anything else). It has to be **POSITED**.

2. HOW ARE THE ETHICAL THEORIES APPLIED?

RELATIVISTS see goodness as relative to culture or experience and so any situation needs to be applied to the relevant cultural value. These may still be very **REASONABLE** but, argues the relativist, even **REASON** is culturally conditioned and not **PURE** as Kant implied.

NATURAL LAW THEORY applies the five primary precepts (acronym **POWER**) to produce the secondary precepts. So the **P** of **POWER** (preservation of life) yields the **SECONDARY PRECEPT** do not abort, do not commit suicide, do not murder. These are not **ABSOLUTE RULES** as we allow killing in time of war. Ultimately the primary precepts are derived from an idea of **HUMAN FLOURISHING** – what it means for a human being to live well or excellently.

KANT sees right and wrong as something irrational, a **CONTRADICTION** or logical inconsistency. There are two types of self contradiction: the **CONTRADICTION IN NATURE** includes suicide and breaking your promises. These cannot be willed universally without contradiction because **EUTHANASIA** if universalised leads to mass suicide of those in pain, and breaking your promise if universalised leads to the elimination of the idea of promising altogether. A **CONTRADICTION IN WILL** is not illogical, but cannot be universally willed or desired. We could never desire not to help our neighbour in distress because we would always want to be helped when we are in distress.

UTILITARIANS see the right action as one that maximises happiness or pleasure. So we need to examine the likely consequences, count how many are affected by our choice, and then apply the Greatest Happiness Principle. We apply utilitarian principles **CONSEQUENTIALLY**.

SITUATION ETHICS argues for a case by case, pragmatic approach that lies somewhere between **ANTINOMIANISM** (no rules) and **LEGALISM** (strict rules). This is a form of Christian relativism espoused by liberal Christians who see the primary command is to love unconditionally (not to judge or make legal demands). Here the person - their needs and desires - is the key. **PERSONALISM** requires we put them first. This can be described as a form of relativism, as Fletcher himself does - he calls it **PRINCIPLED RELATIVISM** because of the one principle or norm - **AGAPE** love, which is absolute and unchanging. But notice there are other definitions of relativism than Fletcher's - who sees goodness as relative to love and to the consequences and situation.

3. REALISM: ARE THE THEORIES TRUE TO HUMAN NATURE?

How realistic are these theories from the perspective of modern sciences such as **PSYCHOLOGY** and **BIOLOGY**?

RELATIVISM fits well the postmodern world where there is no one overarching narrative accepted as true. It also fits **FREUDIAN** psychology where conscience comes from our upbringing and the sense of shame engendered by our parents and teachers. In the postmodern age we are taught to tolerate difference.

NATURAL LAW is often condemned as outdated. However the idea of a shared rational nature is something evolutionary biologists accept. **RICHARD DAWKINS** (The Selfish Gene) talks of a "lust to be nice" coming from our evolved sense of obligation to one another. Is this so different from **AQUINAS**' synderesis rule that we by nature "do good and avoid evil"? Dawkins rejects the **TELEOLOGICAL** nature of Natural Law, as there is no purpose to **EVOLUTION**, he argues, just an endless struggle to survive. But we have inherited an **ALTRUISTIC GENE** from this battle of the genes giving us a shared moral nature. The selfish gene is the self-promoting gene, but for humans, it is in our interest to be moral and so, argues Dawkins, the selfish gene gives us our moral sense and desire to help others.

KANT's ethical theory can be criticised for being **DUALISTIC**. So he sees the world of experience, the **PHENOMENAL** world as opposed to the world of ideas, the **NOUMENAL** world. He also contrasts **REASON** and **EMOTION** in a way that seems to deny moral worth to an action done out of compassion rather than duty alone. The outcome of his theory, that categorical rules are **ABSOLUTE** can also be criticised as unrealistic. In practice we do lie to save someone's life – the goodness is situational, not absolute as Kant suggests.

SITUATION ETHICS suffers from the same two problems as utilitarianism. First, it requires an **IMPARTIALITY** which few are capable of, except Jesus himself. We all tend to rank people according to their closeness to us (family, friends, acquaintances, neighbours and finally strangers). But agape allows no such ranking, otherwise it becomes conditional love. Secondly, it is hard to predict **CONSEQUENCES** and this requires a lifetime of wisdom which few of us possess. William **BARCLAY** (Ethics in a Permissive Society) also points out that social rules embody such wisdom - and those that don't (such as 'homosexuality is wrong') become revised and rejected. But to focus just on individual need and choice is to ignore the important function of rules as guides for us. Ultimately, then situation ethics may be too demanding and so unrealistic.

4. MOTIVATION: WHY BE MORAL?

So we come to the final, and perhaps most pressing question. Why be moral at all? Why not live a life of selfish egoism and be a parasite on the goodness of everyone else?

RELATIVISM is a wide and amibiguous concept. Joseph Fletcher (Situation Ethics) defined himself as a relativist (Situation Ethics is a form of Christian relativism). He argued that we are moral out of love for fellow human beings. But this begs the question why I should bother about fellow human beings when it's not in my interest to do so? Fletcher's answer was that we need to convert to the way of love - commitment comes before action. He calls this **THEOLOGICAL POSITIVISM**. Situation ethics is something of a special case and is arguably not a pure form of relativism as it has one **ABSOLUTE** at its centre - agape love.

NATURAL LAW theorists argue from a **TELEOLOGICAL** standpoint. Be moral, they say, because it is reasonable to want to flourish as a human being – to be the most excellent person you can be. A knife should cut well, says Aristotle, and a human being should be rational in order to flourish well. **AQUINAS** argues that our greatest happiness will be found by aligning the natural law with God's eternal law. This will cause us to be a full, complete human being.

KANT takes the stern, dutiful line of obedience to the moral law or **CATEGORICAL IMPERATIVE**. He argues that rational people will freely choose this way as the most logically consistent way of arriving at the **SUMMUM BONUM**, the greatest good. Autonomous human beings will realise that to obey the categorical imperative out of duty is the best way of building the best of all conceivable moral worlds. Like Kant himself, this moral law within should fill us with awe. It's wonderful. The summum bonum is a mixture of virtue (dutifulness) and happiness ultimately only discovered in heaven (Kant's postulate of **IMMORTALITY**).

UTILITARIANS are not agreed on what motivates us. **BENTHAM** thought we were psychological **HEDONISTS** motivated by the prospect of pleasure and avoiding pain. **MILL** disagreed. He thought pleasure and happiness were not the same, as happiness needed clear goals and strenuous activities. Happiness is to be found in challenges met and difficulties overcome – which sometimes can involve discipline and sacrifice. Why bother with the happiness of others? Mill answered, out of **SYMPATHY** for my fellow human beings. *"In the Golden Rule of Jesus of*

Nazareth" ("do to others as you would have them do to you" Matthew 7:18)", wrote Mill, *"is all the ethics of utility"*.

SITUATION ETHICS requires us to commit to the motive of unconditional love - we accept this by faith (**POSITIVISM**). Fletcher doesn't talk much about motive, but the Bible suggests *'we love because God first loved us' (1 John 4:19)*. So we are motivated by what God in Jesus Christ has first done for us in sacrificing his life for us and suffering pain and humiliation on the cross. Moreover Christ's death liberated us from the slavery to sin and set a new agenda for us - to establish the kingdom of God. This is a kingdom of love. And God gave us the Holy Spirit - the spirit of love in our hearts - to empower us when we find it impossible.

The Night Before the Exam

I have assumed throughout his book that you are an exam candidate, and so I want to write a chapter for you to read the night before the exam, which distills the advice we have been trying to demonstrate here.

Essentially there are two methods of writing essays on Philosophy, Ethics and Christian Thought.

METHOD 1: The thesis approach **TIDE**

In this approach, discussed in the second chapter, we state our thesis (conclusion) early in the first paragraph. We then develop the thesis in the body of the essay, illustrating it briefly and intelligently and presenting contrasting views if we so wish, (which we reject with good reasons). The thesis is then restated in a slightly fuller way (to reflect the careful analysis that precedes it) as a conclusion. **We should use this method when we are confident we understand the question and its implications**.

METHOD 2: The 'ask questions about the question' approach **AQUAQ**

Quite often we may not be very confident about what the question is driving at. If this is the case, then we must adopt the tactic of interrogating the question or asking questions about the question. I suggest we ask three questions and then spend a paragraph answering each one before coming to a conclusion. Each question focuses on one element of the exam question. **We should use this method when**

we are not fully confident about what the question involves.

An example might help here. Suppose I have a question on ethics which asks:

> "The ethical issues around abortion cannot be resolved without first resolving the issue of personhood".

What are the ethical issues surrounding abortion? How and with what ethical tools are these issues resolved? What is meant by the concept of personhood? These three questions (none of which have a single answer), woven into an opening paragraph, give the answer a clear, relevant structure - and the thesis should emerge as we develop our essay. The conclusion is then presented as our own answer to these three questions, perhaps arrived at by contrasting the views of specific philosophers and setting up two ethical theories to see how the idea of personhood is relevant to each.

An equivalent example in Philosophy might address the title "Religious Language is meaningless.", Discuss. The questions you might ask in your opening paragraph might include: What do we mean by religious language? Are there different rules for religious language when compared to everyday language? How is the word 'meaning' to be understood?

When you arrive in the exam room, you must follow the steps set out here. *It is usually a mistake to launch straight into your answer.*

Read every question and highlight key words

Every year candidates make the fundamental error of learning a previous essay off by heart and then regurgitating it in the exam. And every year the examiner complains that candidates did not answer the question. So take a highlighter pen in with you and

1. Highlight all the **trigger/command** words (words like "explain", "to what extent", "discuss"). And then

2. Highlight any words that are **unusual** or unexpected.

If the trigger word is **explain** it is not asking us to **evaluate.** For example "explain the main principles of classical utilitarianism" has the unusual word "classical" in there. By focusing on this word and highlighting it, you are forced to ask the question "what is classical utilitarianism?" and so there is at least a chance that you will avoid the irrelevance of talking about Peter Singer, who is a modern utilitarian.

For Philosophy, sometimes a very specific question is asked to highlight an aspect of an argument, for example, 'Explain Descartes' ontological argument for the existence of God'. It won't gain marks if you go through other ontological arguments as this is not what the question is asking (you could highlight one or two differences, but only to stress the points that Descartes is making). Remember that when a scholar is mentioned in the syllabus, the question can be entirely addressed to that scholar - so the night before go through the syllabus check which scholars might come up.

But (just to be absolutely clear about this) at **A level** we are expected to interweave analysis and evaluation, and this is made clear by trigger words such as "discuss", "assess" or "to what extent".

Sketch out your thesis/ key questions about the question

Always make sure there is some additional loose paper on your desk (put your hand up before the exam starts and request it). Then sketch out quickly your thesis, the main points you need to develop it, and any illustrations you may use. If you are genuinely unsure about the question, don't worry: every other candidate is probably unsure as well. Then use method 2 and ask three questions about the question and impose your own interpretation on it. You will gain credit by this considered and well-directed line which will then emerge as your answer.

My strong advice would be to practise sequencing ideas before the exam, and to have you own mind-map prepared and memorised which you can quickly sketch on a piece of paper as a memory aid.

Be bold in your answer

It's surprising how many candidates come up with statements such as "there are many arguments for and against the ontological argument, and the issue remains difficult to resolve". This is a form of intellectual cowardice which gains no marks at all. Be bold in what you argue, and try hard to justify your approach with good, solid reasons. It is the quality of the argument which gains credit in philosophical writing, not the conclusion you arrive at. Of course, it essential that the conclusion follows.

Analyse, don't just assert

It is tempting to throw down everything you know about, say, utilitarianism in a series of unconnected assertions.

> *"Utilitarianism is teleological, consequentialist and relativistic. It sets up the Greatest Happiness Principle. Utilitarians also believe the end justifies the means."*

These are just assertions which are peppered liberally with what we call technical language (that is language no-one in the real world ever uses). Notice that the above opening few lines demonstrate no understanding and no analytical ability. Instead we should be aiming to write more like this:

> *"Utilitarianism is a theory of rational desire which holds to one intrinsic good: pleasure or happiness. By the greatest happiness principle utilitarians seek to maximise this good in two ways: they seek to maximise net happiness (happiness minus misery) for the maximum number of people. So it is an aggregating theory, where goodness is added up from individual desires to produce an overall maximum good in which "everyone counts as one" (Bentham)."*

You should avoid phrases like 'this famous philosopher' and 'this issue has been debated for centuries'. Is this true? How would we know? Avoid these kinds of broad, sweeping generalisations.

Illustrate your argument

I remember reading an exam report at University which mentioned that one candidate had been highly commended in an essay on utilitarianism for discussing the case of Captain Oates who, during Scott's doomed Antarctic expedition in 1912, walked out of the storm-bound tent in order to sacrifice himself to save his friends, with the words "I may be gone some considerable time". It's an interesting example because it suggests that a utilitarian could be capable of heroic sacrifice rather than the usual illustration candidates give of torturing a terror suspect to find a bomb location.

Spend a few moments working out which examples you will discuss to illustrate key theories and their application. You can pre-prepare them especially in Ethics, and in Philosophy of Religion you can pre-prepare the contrasting arguments which philosophers bring to many of the syllabus areas.

In Philosophy of Religion this advice applies especially to areas such as religious language and the analogies told by Flew (Wisdom's gardener), Hare (three blik illustrations) and Mitchell, (The Stranger), though be concise in how you illustrate these examples - always make them serve the point you are making and not the other way round.

What is the examiner looking for?

In summary the examiner is looking for three things:

Relevance - every sentence linked to the question set and to your main thesis.

Coherence - every sentence and paragraph should "hang together' or cohere. The linkages should be clear as the analysis proceeds.

Clarity - your style should be clear, and in the context, the philosophical vocabulary you use should be clear. You don't necessarily have to define every technical word, but if it does need a little clarification, you can always use brackets for economy. For example:

"Utilitarianism is a teleological (end-focused) theory combining an idea of intrinsic goodness with a method of assessing that goodness by considering consequences".

An example in philosophy would be:

"The Falsification Principle argues that for any statement to be treated as a proposition we must simply be able to deny at least one state of affairs. In contrast the principle of verification requires us to affirm all outcomes by expanding criteria for verification, (and in doing so in our attempt to verify conclusively, 'dying the death of a thousand qualifications', as Flew notes)."

Revision Access Website

Opening March 25th 2018

Our unique guides provide you with a special benefit - your own revision site which is fully integrated with the guides and only available to purchasers.

All our revision materials for Christian Thought, Ethics, and Philosophy of Religion are available to each purchaser of any individual guide. Resources include model essay samples found at the back of each chapter, and also:

- Articles
- Extracts
- Handouts
- Roadmap
- Summary
- Videos
- Whizz Through Powerpoints

Visit: peped.org/revision-access

Postscript - about the author

Peter Baron read Politics, Philosophy and Economics at New College, Oxford and afterwards obtained an MLitt for a research degree in Hermeneutics at Newcastle University. He qualified as an Economics and Politics teacher in 1982. He taught at Tonbridge school from 1982-1991, before training as an Anglican Priest and serving in the parishes of Monkseaton, Newcastle, and Guildford, Surrey. He was Vicar of Holy Trinity, Northwood from 1998-2004. He taught Religious Studies and Ethics at Wells Cathedral School in Somerset from 2006-2012. He is currently a freelance writer and speaker.

In 2007 he set up a philosophy and ethics community dedicated to enlarging the teaching of philosophy in schools by applying the theory of multiple intelligences to the analysis of philosophical and ethical problems. So far over 700 schools have joined the community and over 30,000 individuals use the peped website every month.

www.peped.org contains **EXTRACTS** and **FURTHER READING** mentioned in the exam specification, plus additional articles, handouts and essay plans. Notice that the exam specification merely gives **GUIDANCE** as to further reading - you may use any source or philosopher you find relevant to the construction of your argument. Indeed, if you have the courage to abandon the selection (and any examples) introduced by your textbook, you will relieve the examiner of boredom and arguably launch yourself on an A grade trajectory.

Printed in Poland
by Amazon Fulfillment
Poland Sp. z o.o., Wrocław